THE NEW MANAGER MINDSET

How to Master the Four Secrets
of Leadership that College Doesn't Teach You

Bryan Armentrout
www.newmanagermindset.com

ISBN: 9781520507248

For orders, please reach out to us at
www.newmanagermindset.com
or https://kindle.amazon.com

This book is dedicated to my wife, Beverly
and to author and philosopher Ayn Rand.

Never has one been so patient
and the other so deliberately misunderstood.

ACKNOWLEDGMENTS

Thanks to Megan, Allison, and Nancy for all our help. Your advice and insight are greatly appreciated. A special thanks to those who tolerated my continued experimentation and advice that led to the creation of this system.

Thanks to the team at Self Publishing School - if you have a book in you - do what I did and share it with the world!

But, don't do it alone, get the help you need to be successful.

Self Publishing School

CONTENTS

ABOUT THE AUTHOR

Bryan Armentrout grew up in the wilds of Wyoming. Not many people out there, so it gave him lots of time to ponder the beautiful nature of the world he found himself in.

When he was younger, he wanted to be a chef but has since gone on to become what is known as a Corporate Entrepreneur. This rare skill set allows him to help companies disrupt their status quo and rebuild with the right systems in place. He still loves to cook.

Bryan fell into food quality assurance over 20 years ago and never looked back. At one point in his career, he had responsibility over two divisions within a multibillion dollar dairy company. You most likely have something in your fridge right now that he watched over.

He had the honor of serving as the past Vice Chair for the Safe Quality Foods Technical Advisory Council, a major global food standard. He also helps out with other food safety and risk mitigation programs when he can.

He is very proud of the people he was worked with who have since gone on to bigger and better things. They make it all worthwhile.

Bryan is the CEO of The Food Leadership Group, who specialize in food risk management and meaningful quality systems.

Contact him for a custom analysis of your systems.

https://www.foodleadershipgroup.com/

You can also hire Bryan to speak at your next event:

https://www.bryanarmentrout.com/

He is married and has the good fortune to spend most of this time in Colorado with his wife and their dog. He can also be reached at bryan@newmanagermindset.com, Facebook or LinkedIn.

Thank You

Thank you for reading my book!

I really appreciate all of your feedback and love hearing what you have to say.

I need your input to make the next version even better.

The best way to do that?

Please leave us a helpful REVIEW on Amazon after you have completed reading the book.

Thanks so much!!

~ Bryan

INTRODUCTION
THE NEW MANAGER MINDSET

Productivity is being able to do things that you were never able to do before.

—*Franz Kafka*

Here's a nightmare scenario—

Work has been a confusing mess of conflicting demands and orders from those around you. People stuff your inbox with a river of emails that you try to keep up with all day long—and fail. At the end of another long day, giving up, you prepare to head out the door for your son's soccer game.

Your boss comes running down the hall with a last-minute request for data she needs for a project the CEO requested—tonight. So you sit back down and grind it out. Later on that week, you find out the project was cancelled. So not only did you miss your son's game, but you did all that work for nothing. What a waste of time and energy.

Sound familiar? Has that nightmare scenario ever been a reality for you?

Every day seems like it is filled with random tasks, and every night you go home exhausted and defeated. "Is this how work is done in every company?" you wonder. "If so, how does anyone get anything done?" You know something is wrong, but what is it?

I am here to tell you that you are right. Something is wrong—very wrong.

Is There a Better Way?

Everyone knows that if you want different results, you need to do something differently. The trick is figuring out the difference. I will show you how to take control of this personal chaos and improve your company in the process.

Most people think the CEO is the person responsible for company change. Nothing could be further from the truth. CEOs are isolated from the issues and focused on their own problems. The best person to figure out a solution is you. You are the expert in what you do.

Run Faster!

Is the answer to just "do better" at what you do? Maybe get an MBA? Surprisingly, my experience and research indicate otherwise. Should you take a class or read a book on personal organization or time management? Maybe. These skills can be useful, but all they really do is teach you to run on the hamster wheel we call work-a-little faster—*squeak, squeak, squeak!* These skills do not address the root cause of the problem.

GETTING THINGS DONE

 Most companies have mission and vision statements that are supposed to provide clarity, but they rarely do. They are disconnected from reality. In the real world, most companies are a haphazard collection of processes put in place by people who are no longer there to solve problems that no longer exist. Once I stopped following these rules and changed my mindset, my career skyrocketed.

I am here to help you improve the system that is within your sphere of influence. If you follow my guidelines, your work life will radically change, and you will impact your organization immensely. Your sphere of influence will grow. You will be recognized as a change agent in your company and be known as a problem solver. Good things follow for people who can demonstrate this rare skill set. It is one of the things I always look for when I hire and promote people who work for me.

IS THIS GUY FOR REAL?

What do I know about this? At first, I didn't know anything, I was just like you. All I knew was something was wrong. I made the decision to find out what was wrong—you're going to read all about it! Since then, I have focused on organizational productivity issues at multiple companies for more than two decades. The programs and systems I learned are taken from real-life experiments performed in real-life companies.

I will give you my systems and methods I used to increase productivity and have actually been shown to work. They work because they are derived—not from theoretical methods or how academics think things should work—but from actual trial and error. I have found that most of the assumptions on how to increase productivity through systems and methods are flat wrong. I am presenting my systems and methods for improving not only your work life, but also the work life for those around you.

PROOF POSITIVE

 As an example—and one I'll present in greater detail in Section Four of the book—one company I worked at had issues between two groups of workers. All day long, they would blame each other for the problems they were having, but once we implemented my systems, the issue became clear and the resolution was obvious. Workplace harmony jumped exponentially, and product quality became fantastic. We made a better product and the workers were happy. The plant manager was thrilled, and the workers were too. The New Manager Mindset presented here took me years to figure out. The good news is once I did and saw the way, it was easy to put in place.

I promise that if you follow my principles I will teach you in this book, not only will your workplace become less stressful, but you will also be seen as a person who can get things done. That is a good thing. People who are able to demonstrate this are the people who get raises and promotions—instead of just more work.

LET'S GET STARTED

These systems are easy, and the time to start learning them is now. This process will revolutionize how people look at business, and those who are at the frontline will be known as the experts in the process. Join me on this journey, and decide to improve your life today. Surprise your coworkers when you are the one who sees the path and can clearly articulate it. Leaders are not born—they are created. I will help you become a leader.

The systems in this book were proven time and time again to produce results. The difference here is one of focus and how you choose to improve. You can help yourself by providing a better work environment, and you can also help improve those around you in the process.

The New Manager Mindset is about helping yourself and others achieve the happiness and success everyone deserves.

What is keeping you from starting today?

SECTION ONE
THE PHILOSOPHY OF BUSINESS:
AN ARISTOTELIAN LEAN

The purpose of a moral philosophy is not to look delightfully strange and counterintuitive or to provide employment to bioethicists. The purpose is to guide our choices toward life, health, beauty, happiness, fun, laughter, challenge, and learning.

—*Eliezer Yudkowsky*

A New World

This book is written as a contrarian guide for the new manager or for anyone who supervises people. It provides a set of tools to help you navigate the shark-infested waters of management. It doesn't matter what you manage or what products you have, the rules are the same. I am here to help you succeed.

Unfortunately, the skills that made you a manager are not the skills that will keep you there. You need to learn a new toolbox of skills that allows you to create effective plans and understand those around you in order to succeed as a manager.

The New Manager Mindset is understanding that tools are not the only things you need to succeed in business. Your need to identify a new mindset is what motivated you to seek out this book. You know you need counsel, systems, and a new perspective to achieve far-reaching success as a manager. The book, divided into four sections, with each building on the previous, explores the philosophy of business, consumers, systems, and people and development, and provides example documents and exercises to help you integrate your new knowledge. If you want to be productive as a leader, use your intelligence to do so. Welcome to the team.

THE FIRST STEP

Congratulations, you are a new manager—*now what?* The promotion was sudden and unexpected, but you were always the best worker in the department. Your  husband/wife is so proud. "Hard work *does* pays off," you think to yourself. Indeed it does, and now you have received your just reward.

The only problem is—*what do you do now?* You sit alone in your corporate office; no one is there to help you. HR has given you your tools—a computer, a desk, a phone, and the other basic items that anyone has. You look at the walls, wondering, "What did I get myself into?"

This is normal—and if you are reading this book, you already went through, or are now going through, this stage. You have to learn it for yourself, how to be a manager. No one teaches you; the expectation is that you know how. So people fake it, they try to be like the manager they remember on TV. Maybe they model themselves on another manager in the department. Others try to be like the stereotypical boss that yells at the employee to "work harder!"

It's what you are supposed to do, right?

No, it is not. Your role as boss is one of the most difficult you can undertake. It is a constant challenge, but not like the challenges you tackled in the past. People are promoted because they are good at a task, just like you.

THE STORY BEHIND MY PROMOTION

In my case, what I was good at was microbiology. I was exceptionally good at my job. I could plate bacteria on agar plate media and prep samples faster than anyone. I would take great pride in knowing no matter what the workload was for that week, I could handle it—and I always did.

One day I remember looking at a sample container. One of our main jobs was to test for *Salmonella* in protein powders made at the plants. The first step in the process was to mix the powder with some water in a four-liter jug and incubate it. The bacteria in the powder would grow for a couple of days and come out smelling pretty nasty. You would pull out a sample, put it into a selective media to continue the process. The sample jug would be washed, filled with distilled water, and sterilized and the process started all over again with a new set of samples.

I had now been working in the lab for a couple of years. I learned not many people come into the lab because people are a little leery of what goes on in there. I remember thinking to myself one day, "How many times have I filled, incubated,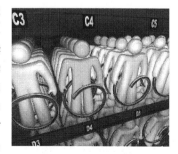

and refilled this particular jug? Hundreds or maybe thousands of times?" Who knew? I just knew I had reached a plateau, and I didn't want to continue down this path.

Working in the lab was fine, but I knew at that moment that if I continued doing what I was doing, it would be my destiny. The only promotion available to me would be the lab manager role, and the current incumbent was young like me, so little chance there. Plus, even if I got a promotion, where would I go from there?

I knew I had to get out, and, in my case, it would be me who would have to make the move.

> Management Mini-Lesson: In order to be promoted, you need to stand out. The first promotion is based on your work ethic. You need to show your skills in getting work done. Once you are promoted, what will keep you there is another skill set.

MY BIG OPPORTUNITY

When my boss noticed my hard work, my opportunity came. I was sent to a plant to cover an opening as a quality assurance manager. It was a small plant, and I didn't have a clue as to what to do. I was put up in a hotel in a small town in the valley in rural California, next to a biker bar. They would party all night, and I would hear what I could only assume were large, hairy men stomping around outside my room in the middle of the night. I propped a chair under the doorknob and hoped they wouldn't kick it in. I didn't sleep too well that first month.

I would get up and go to the plant in the morning, attend

the staff meeting, and try and keep my head down. The plant manager would ask for information I did not have and was not sure how to get. A couple of unpleasant conversations took place, and I am sure he wanted me sent back to the corporate lab as soon as possible. It wasn't looking good.

THE MENTORSHIP THAT MATTERED

Luckily for me, I had a mentor appear at that point. He was the regional quality assurance manager for the company, and if it were not for him, my career advancement potential would have been cut short. He taught me how to be a good manager, how to investigate issues, how to talk to customers, and how to delegate to my team.

Once things turned around, the plant manager was happy to have me on the team. Things changed for me at that point when he asked if I wanted to stay on permanently. My girlfriend at the time was still in Colorado and could not move out, so I politely declined and went back to Denver.

The plant manager wrote a thank you letter to my boss, and she sent it down to me with a note on it that just said, "Good Job." My boss was extremely demanding, and compliments from her were very rare. It was one of the proudest moments of my career. I still have that letter.

The point of this story is this—You don't have to struggle on your own and hope it will all work out. You don't have to pretend and try to figure it out on your own.

Management Mini-Lesson: Don't struggle on your own, hoping it will work out. You need a mentor to help show you the way.

The most important thing my mentor taught me was NOT the actual things I needed to do in my job. It was how to satisfy the plant manager with what he needed to do his job. It was to get an understanding of who was my primary customer in that particular role. It made all the difference, but it was just a start. To really succeed and move beyond it, I needed more. But I am getting ahead of myself, so more on my story later.

PHILOSOPHY OF BUSINESS

Philosophy of Business— really? Isn't philosophy just something that stuffy, old professors with tweed jackets and pipes sitting around in overstuffed chairs talk about in stale libraries on the campus of Harvard or Yale? Hey, I just want to be a good manager.

Philosophy is greatly misunderstood thanks to those types of philosophers, and nothing could be further from the truth. Philosophy is how we live, and, like it or not, we all have a philosophy we live by. It is how we operate in the world and how we understand what is going on around us.

Most people never choose one; it is simply given to them by osmosis or accepted without thought. Our preachers, teachers, friends, parents, and other sources of information contribute their philosophy to us. Do you go to the same church as your parents? Do you hold similar political views to those of your friends? If you don't pay attention, your philosophy can take you in directions you may not want to go.

PHILOSOPHICAL CHOICE

I am here to tell you that you can choose a philosophy to live by—both in life and business. Simply being aware that certain philosophies exist is a big part of the battle. Your business philosophy is a subset of the larger one for your life, but we will limit ourselves to business for the purpose of this book. But know on the personal side, it is there and will influence the business side. When you look at these concepts, they seem simple, but you will be surprised how strongly people can disagree on them. After all, what are two main taboo subjects we avoid in polite conversation? Religion and politics—subjects that are based heavily in personal philosophy.

Here are a couple of quick concepts to get us going:

THE UNIVERSE AND REALITY

The universe is all that is. The universe is reality, and it is everything. There is nothing outside of everything. The universe was here long before you, and it will be here long after you leave. It does not care what you think; it does not care what you do. You are a part of it, not the other way around.

IDENTITY

Things in reality are what they are. They have a nature and behave in a certain way. Fire is hot, water is wet, and a lion is a lion. They are not interchangeable, and each behaves in a predictable manner. Fire cannot be wet, and a lion cannot fly. Things are what they are. This concept was famously put into laymen terms by the ancient Greek philosopher Aristotle when he said, "A is A"—the Law of Identity. He is the guy pictured at the beginning of this section.

Seems pretty basic, right? The universe exists, things that

are in the universe have an identity and are real. You would be surprised when you think about it how many times people forget this. In fact, as you talk with people about what you are learning in this book, they may not even agree with you on these basic rules. Your goal is not to change anyone but only to understand where they come from philosophically when you deal with them. This is good to know, and you will find out why later.

PHILOSOPHY AS A GUIDE

Philosophy is the basic guide you use to understand the world. Reason is the tool you use to figure it out. When we are children, this took the form of asking questions. Who can forget the constant "Why, Why, Why?" questions from children? They are trying to understand the world. Philosophy and reason are the process of understanding and identification.

Two questions swirl around in our heads all day long:

What is it?

What do I do about it?

These questions are our constant companions and teachers in life. They guide us and keep us safe. Their answers are critical to our very survival. If you see a cougar in the woods and you try to pet it because you think it's cute, reality will correct your behavior very quickly.

When our primitive ancestors saw lightning and heard thunder in the sky, they were frightened. They had no comprehension of what was going on. So they asked the questions.

THE FOUNDING OF RELIGION—WELL, MAYBE . . .

Cirroc and Ogg see a flash of lightening and hear thunder rip across the sky on some ancient plain.

Cirroc looks up and asks, "Up in sky, did you see?"

"Yes, and heard too," replies Ogg.

Cirroc looks around, declaring, "I scared, what it mean?"

"I think sky men are angry . . ."

"What they want from us?"

"I don't know, let's try offering some meat and see if works," suggests Ogg.

Our ancient cave-dwelling friends in this scenario go through the same process of identification that we do to this day. We ask questions and then attempt to answer them. This process is constantly playing in our minds.

Their answers may have looked something like this:

Question: *What was it?*

Answer: Lightning and thunder are an expression of anger from the gods. That anger, for some unknown reason, is directed at us.

Question: *What do we do about it?*

Answer: In order to placate the gods, we will provide them with something of value. We will give them a sacrifice to calm them down.

The storm subsided, and the lightning went away—as is the nature of storms. But, in the minds of the cavemen, their sacrifice was the cause of the departure. They made a flawed connection in their thinking. They linked the storm passage with the offering. They now believed the two had a cause-and-effect relationship. Now that they had this relationship established, they thought they had the power to influence what the gods wanted.

QUESTIONS LEAD TO MORE QUESTIONS

Once that connection was made, more questions were asked. People who heard the story wanted more information. None was available, so stories were written to provide insight into the sky men. The gods became simply more powerful versions of people, with a lot of the same vices. Some were cruel, some were playful, others cared about man and were helpful. Each one had different powers that controlled different aspects of nature.

The water in the ocean goes in and then back out over the course of a month. Who controls that? Well, a god of the sea must do that. So, another god was born to explain a particular phenomenon. Temples were built, and people specialized in their study. Religion was born.

The easiest way to think of religion is as a form of philosophy. It is an attempt to explain the universe. People were just trying to answer the two questions listed above. The answers they got gave them the system they created. Disputes over the answers to these types of questions caused splits in the branches, and new religious groups were born.

The point here is not for me to persuade you in any particular direction. It is simply to bring awareness. Knowledge is seeing and observing. This is how we operate, and philosophy is the system we all use to see the world, whether we consciously recognize it or not. It is the lens that we see through when viewing reality.

I bring this to your attention to show you how primal reasoning is for us. It is who WE are. It is how the human race operates, and our ability to reason is what separates us from every other animal on this planet. It is our ability to think. It is also what will take you to the next level in your new role as a leader and manager of people.

YOUR PHILOSOPHICAL BELIEF SYSTEM

If you understand this concept as a starting point, you are ahead of almost every other person around you. Most of us had our beliefs instilled in us by other people. We've been taught like this going back to our cavemen days as to why things are the way they are. But the universe does not care, the rules of the game are always there, and it is our job to figure them out.

As we advance as a species in our knowledge, things previously unexplained become clear. We now know what causes lightning and thunder. We know and can even predict where it will occur. We know why the ocean tide goes in and out. Sacrifices to angry men in the sky are not needed and never were. We move forward.

What does all this mean for you? It is important to know reality has an identity and things are what they are. Machines, people, and processes operate under a set of rules. It is our job to figure out what they are—in reality.

What is it?

What do I do about it?

Many a person has fought against reality—and they always lose. They build castles in the sky; they create systems and ideas not based on the facts, but on what they *think* things should be. They want their explanations to be true, even if they are not. This is one of the biggest mistakes you can make, but it can be very hard to see. Remember, the key to this is reality. It is the one thing that is the true measure of what should be. Reality is always there and so are the answers it provides.

Most systems and ways of looking at the world are based

on false assumptions. Think of our caveman friends—they saw an unexplainable phenomenon and attributed an answer to it that was wrong. This example is simplified and most likely not how it happened, but for purposes of illustration, an entire belief system was built around it. Once you are caught in such a view, it is very hard to get out.

If you cannot use reality as the gauge for the truth of your beliefs, you are lost. You have taken yourself out of using reality as your base of knowledge. This is a very dangerous place to be.

THE PHILOSOPHIES OF OTHER PEOPLE

The people you work with are people. They are just like you, and they have a nature. They have an identity. They have a way of operating and can be predictable to a certain degree. This degree of predictability is often in direct correlation to their orientation to reality. The more rational a person is, the more predictable their behavior is. This is important to recognize in others. If you work with an angry person who is hard to understand, you need to see this in them and recognize it for what it is.

Most people will try to force their views of things onto other people. If that view is based on a false set of beliefs, reality cannot be appealed to. Unfortunately, a lot of people in this situation may still try to force others to conform to their wishes.

What is really curious is that two main views of the world, created thousands of years ago, dominate how we view the world to this very day and can be traced back to their teachings.

Dueling Philosophers

Aristotle and Plato are two of the most important philosophers in history. Aristotle was actually a student of Plato. Both men said many great things, but the difference here is the one we need to focus on.

Aristotle held a different view of reality than his teacher did. He believed things were knowable and had a nature. His shorthand way of saying this was with the phrase "A is A," called the Law of Identity. That is, a thing is what it is. It has a specific nature and is knowable. This is the reality-based orientation we have been talking about so far.

 Plato, on the other hand, believed reality and the world were just a shadow. A cat was a shadow of the "form" that is the source of all cats in this world. This "form" lives in another dimension that we cannot know. Individual cats are simply different manifestations of the "form" projected into the world. He believed the things we see are not real and another dimension beyond ours actually held the real things.

Remember, he had no actual evidence of this view. He could not point to a "form" or provide proof that we could see. He placed it all out of our reach and made it up to explain what he thought needed an explanation.

The point here is not to give a history of philosophy but to illustrate these two very different views of the world. One that is real and one that is but a shadow referencing a real world we cannot know. These two views are around us every day, as are their implications. The purpose of this book is not to get into those schools of thought in detail, but if you want to learn more, I suggest you study both of these giants. For now, this is sufficient for our purposes.

Is the universe knowable and understandable? Or is it

unreal and simply shadows of what really is? Your answers to these types of questions guide your life and how you live it. These types of thoughts guide you in ways you are not aware of. Bringing them to the surface is an important first step. Play with it a little, ask yourself why you believe what you believe. The answers may surprise you.

What do I know?

How do I know it?

How Ideas Build on Each Other

Philosophy leads to an approach that is hierarchical in nature. This means that previous ideas build on each other—and it never stops. We begin in childhood and continue to build on our knowledge for our entire lives, stacking information on top of other information and making new connections as we go. Knowledge must have reality as its base if the pyramid is to be sound.

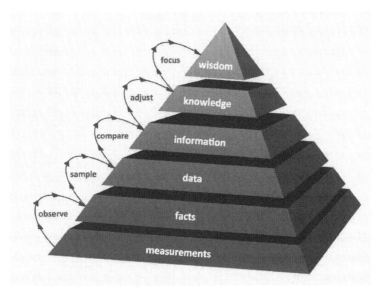

Concepts are born out of this stacking. Concepts are

simply things grouped together. We can point to an individual you know. You can see him in reality, but you cannot point to the idea of "father." It is a concept of a male individual who has produced a child.

It is built upon prior knowledge and what you have learned in the world. It is important to remember that you can trace the concept back to reality. It has a starting point. Concepts are a way to allow us to think about higher things. If we had no term for things like "father," we would be unable to expand our knowledge of the universe.

Numbers are a concept, too. Just like the above example, you cannot point to the concept "fifteen" in the world. You can point to thirteen birds on a wire, but it is very difficult to hold all that in your mind. The number "15" is a concept for the entities in their place. Without the concept, the brain cannot function on a higher level.

Which is the easier concept to hold in your mind?

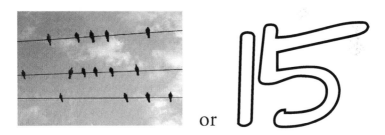 or

You have to actually count the birds, which takes time. The concept of "15" is independent of the birds and can refer to any fifteen items. It is a concept.

To bring this point home, philosophy needs to be based on reality and needs to use reason and logic to build a hierarchy of knowledge in order to successfully live in the world.

LIFE AS A MANAGER HAS A STARTING POINT

You are now a manager and at a critical point in your career. The skills that got you here are not the skills that will take you to the next level. People advance because they were good at a task. You were the fastest and most efficient at what you did.

That's great, but it serves little purpose in your new role. You know that now. You now need to lead people, not do things fast. Most people who are promoted simply try to apply their old skills to their new job by making other people do things faster. This is not why you are in your new role. Your job is to support them and to give them the tools to do their job, not do it for them.

The context of your new position is like your life, your world starts when you are born. It is the same at your company. Your work life starts at the point you begin. You have no knowledge of what came before or why. Others have been there longer and have a different understanding based on when they started. People who join your team after you will not have your context, but it all shapes how you approach your role. Things were done for a reason. Those reasons may no longer be valid. Find out before you leap in and start tearing things apart; otherwise you may cause more damage than good.

WHY YOUR BOSS IS SO IMPORTANT

Your boss is the most important person in the company. This person makes or breaks your career within the company. If you work for a good  boss, things are generally good even if the company itself is not so great. If the boss is bad, there is little you can do to improve your situation. Keep this in mind as it cannot last like this for long. Eventually you will need to either find a new boss or find a new job.

Most new managers feel it is their role to control everything. Not possible. The ironic thing is that if you are a good leader, you control less. You trust your team to do their job and allow them the flexibility to do it in a way they are comfortable with. Give them the keys, tell them where you want them to go, and then let them drive. If they need help, they will ask, and if it turns out that they are an employee you shouldn't have trusted with the keys, you need to find out sooner rather than later.

Management Mini-Lesson: To be an excellent manager means you will control your team LESS and, instead, support them, allowing them the needed flexibility, to do their jobs.

THE WHY OF A COMPANY

Based on his book, *Start with Why*, Simon Sinek gave an excellent TED Talk on the "why" that a company needs to be successful. I have attached a link to a YouTube presentation at the end of this book. In the talk, Sinek discusses three main areas that I think compare to what we are talking about in this section of the book.

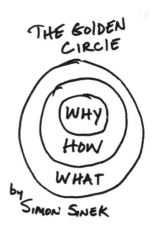

THE GOLDEN CIRCLE

WHY
HOW
WHAT

by SIMON SINEK

Why –   The Purpose

What –   The Process

How –   The Result

Like a business, you also have your own answers for these questions. They are the starting point for everyone, and you need to first find out your why. Why are you doing what you do? This is your philosophy of business.

Your why is the most important of these questions. Why do you want to be a manager? Is it just to make more money? If so, your chances of making it very far in your career are limited.

Just like the reason you were promoted, you think doing things faster is going to get you more money. You actually need to teach your team how to do things, and then you can multiply what you can do through your team.

Management Mini-Lesson: Figure out your "Why"— why do you want to be a manager?

This is why objectives and goals are so important; they lay out a plan of how you need to approach your role. The interesting thing is they are very rarely linked to a company mission or vision statement. This is because the philosophical approach to business is not used. In most cases, vision statements have not taken an Aristotelian approach and end up with a mishmash of vague phrases and words that do not apply to what anyone does. The vision and mission statements are shadows of some actual meaning in another realm.

MISSION STATEMENTS—AND REALITY

Here is the mission statement from Enron: "Respect, Integrity, Communication, and Excellence."

Enron was a 111 billion-dollar company and employed over 20,000 people at its peak in 2000. It was found that the company had systematically cooked the books, hiding bad investments and losses by using fraudulent accounting methods. They went bankrupt in December 2001 and were the reason for the Sarbanes-Oxley Act of 2002.

What the hell does this mission statement have to do with anything? We can see it was completely removed from reality. This company was run by criminals! Their mission statement was simply a collection of nice-sounding words that gave no direction. We see what happened to this company, and the fact they thought this was a good mission statement was part of the problem.

To paraphrase what we have been talking about, two main views of the world and of business are in place. It is my contention that in order to be an effective manager (and person for that matter) you need to have an Aristotelian view of the world and of your role.

Aristotelian: Reality is what it is. People and things are knowable and understandable. It is your job to figure it out, using logic and reason to do so.

Platonic: Things are only shadows of the real world and not as they appear. We cannot know the real world and must try and guess what reality truly is.

Now which of these views shaped Enron's mission statement? Once you see this, you can see how philosophy shapes your view of the world and how you approach it. If you understand this, it allows you to be a very effective manager.

Now, here is an example of what I consider to be a good mission statement:

Google's mission is to organize the world's information and make it universally accessible and useful.

Yes, it is their mission–and anyone who reads this knows their mission. It makes sense, and you can support it. It's not long, and it doesn't contain buzz words or pander to shareholders. Beautiful.

If you use logic and reason to manage your activities and how you approach the world, it is refreshing for other people who actually deal with you. You are now predictable and understandable, and people are attracted to that. You will be known as someone who is professional and able to get things done. More importantly, you will be someone who can figure out what are the right things are to get done.

Management Mini-Lesson: By making logic and reason the philosophical base in how you approach your role as manager, you will reap success—both for yourself, your team, and your company.

PEOPLE AND THEIR STYLES

People are what they are–and they have a personality style. Many books, classes, quizzes on Facebook and other places have been created to put people into categories. What is the best way to think about the people you deal with? You can spend a lot of time learning Briggs Myers and other systems, but people only have tendencies and people in the middle can switch back and forth. Not much help when you are trying to find the best way to work with them.

The most important aspect in my opinion is a person's source of energy. Extroverts tend to get their energy from being around other people. They typically love being in crowds, going to sporting events, and talking to everyone at the company picnic. Introverts, on the other hand, tend to be drained by such things. They mostly get their energy by being alone and contemplating things. They dread the idea of being at the game and talking with people.

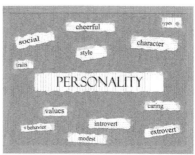

Extroverts often have a hard time understanding introverts and may think something is "wrong with them." They may think introverts are aloof or snooty if they don't want to chat for ten minutes in the breakroom or cringe a little bit when an extrovert comes into their office uninvited. However, nothing could be further from the truth. Introverts simply need their alone time, and if someone wants to come into their space, they need permission. If it is a good time, an introvert is happy to have you join them for a while in their world.

Once again, this is simply reality. People are who they are and need to be dealt with in these terms. If you can realize this, you will go a long way with people, and they will respect your courtesy and professionalism. Later in the book, you will find how critical this is and why so many people who don't recognize this attribute fail in their job.

> Management Mini-Lesson: Recognize your colleagues' styles of functioning at work and in the world. Knowing and respecting their styles will bring you success with them thus helping you, your whole team, and your company.

BLIND SPOTS

I took a leadership course once that taught me an important lesson. People have blind spots. They have things they do or ways they act that may be an issue when dealing with others. For me, I have the subconscious habit of scowling when I am concentrating at a computer. I am not doing it on purpose; it is simply the way my face looks to others when I am concentrating. I learned at this class that people who walked by my office interpreted this as a bad mood, so they should steer clear of me.

I was subconsciously saying to everyone who saw me, "Stay the hell away!" and they did. Will I be able to change this behavior? Most likely no, and I am probably scowling at my screen right now as I write this book. What I can do is recognize the behavior and let  people know about it. If they understand this is my "working face" and it simply means I am concentrating, the confusion goes away. A lot of times this process of self-awareness cannot be initiated by you; others need to tell you.

This is why getting feedback from your team is so important, not only on things that need to be done, but on communication and management skills as well.

Management Mini-Lesson: Create opportunities for your team to give you feedback to help you figure out your blind spots in order to clear confusion and create more understanding.

How to Organize Your Work

Your focus is all you have. You need to choose every day what it is you should focus on. The best book I have read on the subject is David Allen's *Getting Things Done—The Art of Stress-Free Productivity*. It will help you organize your work, but what I am talking about in this book is a level above. Knowing why you are working on things will lead to the "what" and "how" of doing them.

Every day I start off with a "to-do" list on what I need to get done that day. This is written from a list of things I want to get done that week. The weekly list tends to be a little more aspirational, and I put more things on there than can get done. That's okay; these are things I want to get done and need to be at the front of my mind without taking up space there. These then tie into the objectives for my department and how we interact with other departments.

A whiteboard in your office is critical to this process. It allows you to visually keep track of what you are working on in a way you can look at every day. In addition, everyone who walks in your office can see it as well. They know what you are working on.

> Management Mini-Lesson: Create a clear system of articulating and reminding yourself (and even your team) of your goals—your daily, weekly, and even your longer-term goals.

Who Can You Control?

In reality, very few people. You can really only effectively manage five to seven people directly. It's too much time and effort to manage more than that because you can't give them the attention they deserve. So, everyone else you come into contact with is beyond your direct control. You need to influence these others in order to get things done. You do this by understanding their needs first and then communicating yours to them.

Find a Way for Both Sides to Win

A recent example may provide some light on what I am talking about. I started a new job, and one of our major manufacturing partners was not on the best of terms with us. I work in food manufacturing, and one of the things companies do is utilize other companies to help them manufacture products.

If you need cheese made in California for the market under your brand name, and you don't have a plant in the area, another company can make it for you. This is called co-packing. Some companies specialize in doing this for other companies, and it's all they do. They operate on your behalf and go through an approval process to do so. The downside is they are not part of your company and may have a slightly different way of doing things.

If you take an approach that is reality-based, you realize you cannot just bend them to your will. Even if you could, they would resent you for it and find other ways to undermine your efforts. You have to understand the rationale of why they do what they do. This, of course, assumes they are operating from a rational and reality-based focus in the world, just as you do. If they don't, they are most likely not going to be a good partner, and the relationship will continue to be filled with conflict and strife. Find a way to change the relationship or get out of it if you can.

If two parties cannot rely on reality and reason to come to a mutual understanding, you have nowhere to go. If they hold a skewed view of reality, no common ground can be reached. Your only alternative is to try and force them to your point of view. This is the source of much of the pain and suffering in the world. Why are you working with them in the first place?

Management Mini-Lesson: You can't bend another party, whether it be a colleague, employee, or partner company, to your will. Instead, frame the interaction so both sides benefit.

The correct way to frame the discussion is to make sure both sides win. In order for the trade to be beneficial, both parties need to benefit. Find a way to do this, and you will find a solution.

Once you find this common frame of reference, it is not you against them and their view; it is both of you working toward a common goal in reality.

My Big Opportunity, Continued

Earlier in this section, we talked about my big break and how it came about. As a microbiologist, I knew I had to do something different if I wanted to get promoted. By taking a risk and working in the plant, I showed my boss I was willing to learn new skills and I wanted to be promoted. Things don't always happen right away, but taking that risk showed upper management I was one of the 10% who was willing to grow. I could demonstrate an adaptability and willingness to succeed. I had successfully navigated the waters as a QA manager and returned to corporate headquarters proud of my accomplishment.

But—I still went back to the lab. Really? They didn't have a shiny, new job waiting for me? Nope. I had to make sure to let my boss know I was grateful for the experience and was ready for more. When they had the right opportunity, I was ready to take that on as well. That took about four months to develop.

A new role was created in the company due to growth, and I was asked if I would like to take on this new challenge. In this job, I would manage the technical and customer service functions for the company in the ingredient business. It would be a challenging position, working with four other people who were managing the business. This was a major change in my role, which I accepted with a bit of uncertainty. If you want to grow, you need to step out of your comfort zone.

We all know the story of Little Miss Muffet—sitting on her tuffet and eating curds and whey, but what the heck is "whey"? When cheese is made, you have liquid that is left over, also known as whey. The whey is not just water; it contains a lot of minerals and proteins that didn't get captured in the cheese and lactose (milk sugar). This whey is then dried as is or is separated into protein and lactose sugar before drying.

We managed this business. When whey is made, it is a byproduct of the main process, cheesemaking. As a result, you don't always know how much you have to sell. You make cheese to sell; you don't make whey in order to have cheese. So, forecasting how much cheese you are going to make translated into how much whey you had to sell. This was offered in quarterly contracts.

The year I started in this job, the forecast for cheese manufacturing was really off. The prediction for cheese sales was too high, and we sold a lot less cheese than expected, a whole lot less. Suddenly we had no whey powder to sell, which meant many customers had contracts with us to purchase a product that did not exist.

INTO THE LION'S DEN

I just started in the department and spent my day answering calls from angry customers wanting to know where their product was. We had none to sell, the warehouses were empty. Other than bodybuilders, no one eats whey powders from cheese directly. They go in other products like sports drinks, candy, snacks, soup mixes, and similar products. So, we were shutting down manufacturing for other companies in the process. This was a huge crisis. I wasn't sure if I was going to have my new job for very long.

I applied the principles in this section to the issue at hand. I was just learning them at this stage in my career, but I understood enough to make these powerful concepts work to find a solution to the issue.

I thought about it and looked at the reality of the situation. Lying to customers and telling them the product was going to be ready soon would stop them from yelling at me for a little while, but reality would be back soon enough. The short-term gain was irrational and not something I would even consider.

I did know the lack of whey would not last forever. It was just a temporary lull in the sales stream, an unanticipated dip that would return to statistical averages soon enough. By looking at past data, I could see this trend and extrapolate that this may have been one of those dips that showed up without warning every now and then. I confirmed this by talking to the cheese sales team.

So, I put together a plan. Cheese production hadn't stopped; it had just slowed down. Whey was still being manufactured, just not as fast as we needed it. I looked at our customer base to identify the biggest ones—the customers that supplied whey powder to some of the biggest food companies in North America. Shutting them down would be a disaster. I looked at our available inventory and then presented a plan to my boss. She agreed, and we put it into action.

I reached out to this core group and explained the situation. Whey powders were limited, and we were going on allocation. Some customers would receive a portion of their contract, but others would receive none. The larger customers would normally get multiples of truckloads a month. They were cut back to just enough to keep their key customers running and meet orders. They were not happy, but they understood the situation and everyone in this category was being treated in a similar manner. Fairness was critical to the success of this plan.

The more difficult group to contend with was the smaller traders or brokers who were not going to get any product. The same scenario was explained to them, but we had to explain that until we returned to normal, no product would be available. They also understood and used stock or secondary channels to get through the storm. They knew this would blow over and business would continue.

Things did return to normal in a few months, but it was

stressful. As soon as loads were ready, they were out the door with no time to spare. No one sued anyone, and it went as smoothly as could be expected.

THE AFTERMATH

Several years after this happened, my boss and I reminisced about this incident. In retrospect, she said she was surprised that I put together this plan and presented it to her. These were her customers, not mine, and she was a little insulted that I took this initiative. But, I was right, and it was a good plan. It was the reasonable thing to do, and it balanced the needs of all parties in a fair manner.

I was a little shocked when she told me this. At the time, it never occurred to me that I was overstepping my bounds by putting this proposal together. If I had executed it on my own, this story would not have had a happy ending, but at the time I was at least smart enough to know that I needed to get consensus for the plan.

What is the moral of the story? Well, it's a simple but an important one. By recognizing reality and the situation in relation to the rational best interest of the parties involved, I was able to put together a plan that worked. It worked because it was a reflection of what was actually happening and it relied on using my mind to face reality and see what was happening. Although we haven't worked together in years, my previous boss and I are friends to this day.

WHAT ARE THE MANAGEMENT LESSONS HERE?

Things are what they are. It is our job to understand them and use reason and rationality to find a solution that is best, given the context of the situation. Knowledge is always based on the facts available at the time. If new facts in relation to reality become known, either through a search for understanding or a change of circumstances, that's great. But, you were NOT wrong in the previous situation. Knowledge has a context and is hierarchical in nature. Facts build upon themselves and may take you in unexpected directions. New information builds on what was known before. You were not wrong, you just know more now within that context.

I grew in my role at this cheese company, and I expanded my knowledge of the business. It was a fascinating time. We had factories all over the country, and customers all over the world. It was a fast-paced and challenging environment. However, it was not always easy. I was about to learn a major lesson about dealing with people.

LEARNING THE HARD WAY

My growth brought me into contact with another key figure, and this time it was not for the positive. I worked with an individual who created the forecast for the whey business. He was friendly but, as I soon found out, not on the same philosophical page as I was. He took the opposite approach, at least from my perspective. He believed things were not as they appeared and they could be changed if one wanted. He spent a lot of time denying reality and attempting to mold the world to his view of it. Sound like a philosophical approach we know?

He would give me numbers for the quarter on production and anticipated volumes. I would use these for sales and how much product we would be able to offer our customers based on the cheese production. I knew enough about the business to anticipate the nature of the product and knew not to oversell product to customers. I did not want to go through a shortage like we'd had before.

My first experience with his views came when the first quarter working with him was coming to a close. Much to my surprise, the forecast was really wrong. It was way under, and I had an unexpected shortage of product on my hands. This was exactly what I had hoped to avoid. Angrily, I went down to talk with this person to find out what the hell had happened. He had given no notice, and based on what I was seeing in the production reports, this was something that was known a month or more prior.

The response I received was not what I expected. It was a complete denial that any of the issues even existed and our previous planning process was not what he remembered. As we recreated the process to determine where things went wrong, it was as if we had entered a courtroom and he were on trial.

"I never said that. I didn't do that. You can't prove it," he repeated time and time again. These were things he said and, they were things he did. His defense is what I have come to find as one of the most important discoveries of my career at that point. My recognition of what he was doing from a philosophical perspective was very important. He was denying reality, saying I couldn't prove what he had said or he had promised what he said.

I went away after the conversation not mad, just confused. I pondered his reaction for a long time. I had come across it before. I came to realize in time what he was doing, and then it made sense. It was irrational, but at least I could understand where it was rooted.

THE CONCEPT OF THE BURDEN OF PROOF

An important concept in logic is the concept of who has the burden of proof. When someone makes a claim, they always have the duty to defend their position. It is not your job to disprove their statement.

This is the same as in a trial. If you are accused of a crime, the State is required to prove you are guilty. You are not required to prove you are innocent. This is very important and not readily apparent. When a trial is complete, you are either judged to be guilty (the State proved you did it) or not guilty (the State failed to prove you did it). You are *not* shown to be innocent. Why? Because your goal was not to prove your innocence; it was the State's goal to prove you were guilty. Your innocence is not the question at hand, but most people think it is.

If we had a system where the State could accuse you of any crime, and you had to prove you were innocent, it would be insanity. They could say a murder took place in Florida last week. The police know you live in Colorado, but it is very easy to get on a plane and go to Florida. A person matching your description was seen leaving the crime scene. They decide to charge you with the murder of the man in this case. This all takes place without your knowledge. The first hint you get is when you see a helicopter out your back window and FBI agents surrounding your house.

They kick in the front door and drag you away, charging you with the murder in Florida. You hire an attorney to help you prove you did not kill this man. You have to prove you were somewhere else. If you fail to show your innocence, you will be sent to jail for no less than thirty years—or worse. Have a nice day.

If this were our system, the win/loss record for the prosecutor would be perfect, but a lot of innocent people would be in jail. It would be in their best interest to find the most unlikely person to accuse of the crime because they would have the smallest chance of proving their innocence.

My Defense

Back to our story on the whey forecast. I now understood—this is how he operated. He viewed it as my job to prove he said or did something, and, if I failed to do so, he was innocent. Once I understood this, I had to take a defensive stance. I wrote down everything we discussed, took meticulous notes, and kept copies of all emails and reports for forecasting. I created a paper trail to prove that he said or did something on a particular date or time. This was a very inefficient and unproductive way to do my job, and it impacted my productivity as well.

Eventually, this brought his behavior to light. It became clear to his boss that he was not performing his job and was causing issues, so he was eventually let go from the company. He was a nice guy, and I had nothing against him. But he was fighting reality and creating a false world to live in. He couldn't even see it, and it eventually cost him his job.

Management Mini-Lesson: The way we choose to see the world is important and often overlooked. The only person you can control is you—how you react and how you choose to deal with other people. People have natures, so if you need to, define how you to react to them in that context.

Everyone has free will. In order for us to survive in the world, you need to use your mind. It is our tool of survival. We do not have to think, but if we choose not to, reality will be there to exact a toll for that choice.

PHILOSOPHICAL DECISION-MAKING

What is the purpose of this section, and why is it in the book? Let's go over an example of what I am talking about.

The Example: You are working at the corporate headquarters, and this is your first week on the job. Things are settling in, and you have a nice office with a view of the river. "This is why I worked so hard. This is fantastic," you think to yourself. A member of your team taps his knuckles on the door and gives you a look that tells you something is up.

"You got a sec?" asks Bob in a manner that says it's a good thing you are sitting down.

"Sure, come on in," you reply.

"We've got a problem, and it's a big one," Bob divulges. Bob has been with the company for 13 years. He has worked in the operations group the entire time. He's a nice guy who does what is expected, but little more than expected.

"Tell me about it," you respond as you motion for him to sit down at your desk.

"I just heard from the plant in Corning, New York. They are testing product and finding some defects in the optical lenses we are making. They are not serious defects, and the plant wants permission to ship them. Orders are due to go out first thing in the morning, and if we miss this order with the customer, they are going to drop us as a supplier. The plant says the customer will most likely not see the defect or will miss it during inspection, so it's not a big deal. I heard the divisional vice president has already said we should take the chance and ship. What should we do?"

These types of decisions come up all the time in management. People make assumptions, and they assign outcomes that may or may not be true. They appeal to authority to push you in a direction that may not be right. What should you do?

Most people believe your role as a manager in scenarios such as this is to sit in the chair and make the call on your own. But, in most cases, the decision is really just the one they want you to make and not your own. They want you to take the responsibility and the blame if it goes south. It may seem easy in the moment, but it is not how you want to do things. Resist this temptation—you most likely have more time to make the decision than you are being led to believe.

You need to find the facts. First, call the plant and actually talk to people to find out what is going on. You need data if you are going to make a decision. Because of the pressure of the situation, the information you are given at that moment is most likely wrong or incomplete. Reality is what is, and you need to find out what that is. Don't react to the first thing you are told, because it is usually wrong.

If you cannot go see for yourself, find out as much as you can. This may be a much bigger or smaller situation than you realize based on current facts. The surprising thing most people do not realize is that in almost every situation, you do not need to make a decision at that exact moment. It is almost always better to wait a bit, widen your perspective, and gather more information. The higher the pressure to make a decision, the more important this becomes.

Management Mini-Lesson: In most situations, it is better to wait, gather the facts (the reality), and process a situation with your team than to make emotional snap-decisions.

"Okay, let's call the plant and get the facts," you calmly reply.

Your demeanor in situations such as this will build your reputation in the company. If you become emotional and angry, you make the situation worse. Emotions are good, and they are reflections of what your mind considers important, but they are not how you guide your life. I am not saying to deny your emotions; just don't use them to make your decisions.

Once you call the plant, you come to realize that some minor defects are indeed in the lenses. They are random and the plant estimates 9% of the production lot is impacted by the issue. The entire run is on hold, and the quality inspection programs and an operator who noticed the defect during the run were key in finding the issue. Congratulate them for their diligence.

You gather a team to look at the issue. The very next thing you need to ask yourself is whether or not this defect is something that will impact the customer. You may think you know, but in many cases you are unsure. That's okay because, more often than not, the customer-facing divisions in the company, such as sales, do not know either.

The data is in. The product review is complete. An investigation is under way to determine the cause. Great, what do you do next?

"Okay, guys, let's get the sales team involved and present the facts. Our next step is to call the customer," you announce to the team as you lean back in your chair. A couple of people glance at each other across the table.

Actually call the customer and admit you made a mistake? Yes, in this scenario, this is exactly the right thing to do. The reality of the situation is there—and it is sitting in the warehouse ready to be loaded on trucks.

You arrange a conference call and explain the situation to

the customer. It turns out that once the defect is explained, it actually will not cause an issue on their end. These lenses will be repolished at their factory prior to the installation process, so the defect will be removed. You ask if it is okay to ship the product, and they agree to the shipment. Corrective actions are put in place at the plant after the investigation reveals a shaping blade was misaligned and caused the defect.

The customer is impressed. Your professionalism is evident and your credibility—as well as your company's—just went up. You could have shipped, and the defect may have not caused an issue with the customer. But you didn't know it at the time. You didn't have that fact and your decision would have been based on deception and hoping the customer would not find the defect. Not only that, your team sees how you make decisions and know something was wrong. You would think that making snap decisions based on your authority is what managers do, but you couldn't be more wrong.

WHAT IS RIGHT WINS IN THE LONG-RUN

Do you see the difference? One approach is facing reality head-on, understanding the facts, and going where they take you. What if you found the defect would cause an issue and you shouldn't ship? You will miss the order and the customer will be mad? They may be, but you the right thing and they will still respect you for it. Reality will show you the correct path because when two people have a different interpretation of the facts of reality, one is right and one is wrong.

Management Mini-Lesson: Exceptional managers let reality make their decisions.

WRAPPING IT UP

In summary, philosophy has an enormous impact in all you say and do. It is how you think, and it is how others think and interact with you. If you understand this, you have a gigantic edge on how you handle situations and how you react. You are not driven by your emotions and unsure of what to do; you can use your mind to figure out what to do. Your reputation will grow very quickly, and you will be known as someone who can get things done.

 The world is real, and it is knowable. Our tool of survival is our mind, and reason is how we deal with the world. You can try to force others to do what you want or try to fool them into doing it, and it may work for a while in the short run, but you will not succeed in the long run.

Existence is king, and identity is the calling card of everything in it. Your identity is known to anyone who interacts with you, so make sure that what you put out there is consistent with reality. If you are consistent, everyone will know how you react and how you manage situations. This important secret is one of the keys of successful management.

Everyone you work with should know what you will do even before you say it. This is based on reality, and it is amazing once you get to this point. You will be known as reasonable, fair, and professional.

People will come to you for decisions because you will make them based on reality and the needs of the business—and not on some hidden agenda or blurred understanding of the situation.

THE KEY TAKEAWAYS

- You need to consciously have a philosophy for your approach to business.

- The rational approach is reality-based.

- Your tools for understanding reality are reason and logic.

- Base your plans and decisions on the facts of reality, and you will succeed in the long run.

Do you see a pattern here? These concepts are simple, but they are not simple to implement. They require constant focus and attention. That is why you are a manager. You are a manager to use your mind, and that is what the company is paying you for. Use it to see reality, use it to understand the issues you face, and use it to understand those around you and how they operate.

You will find very few people in your office do this. If you doubt me on this, bring this up over lunch one day with a coworker and see how they answer these questions:

1. Is my reality the same as yours?

2. Is there anything more important than reason and logic for solving problems?

3. When a problem happens, who should solve it?

I suggest you only do this sparingly because the answers you get will shock you. Some people will have no answers, and others will simply defer to the will of the group for decisions or authority. Other people will have no idea or will jump from topic to topic, unable to integrate their thinking. These types of conversations can be very revealing, and you will find it actually scares some people.

Action Plan: Decision Awareness

Simply becoming aware of decisions can provide valuable insight. Write down the following questions and take them with you during your day. As decisions come up, write them down and answer the questions.

- What was the decision?
- Who asked you to make a decision?
- What was the reason for the decision?
- Why was the decision important?
- How will this decision impact you and those around you?
- What impact does this have on the consumer of your product or service?
- When does this decision need to be done by?
- What would happen if you did nothing?

Do this for two weeks. At the end, take a look and see if you can find any patterns. Are your decisions based on your reasoning or are you being asked to implement decisions from others? What do you base your decisions on?

This exercise points out the New Manager Mindset—a philosophical approach that will serve you no matter what you do and what your responsibilities are. We are all in reality, and these rules apply to everyone.

This exercise is meant to help you see the process—both the process at your business and your decision-making process, too—because recognition is half the battle. If you want to develop a New Mindset, you need to start by thinking differently.

Congratulations! and Up Next

You are now starting to understand philosophy and its application in business.

This section puts you ahead of 99% of the people around you. No one thinks about this - they just go about their jobs expecting things to just work out. That gives you a tremendous advantage in your career and in your life. The information in this section is just an outline. Like most things worth learning in life, you must continue your education if you want to grow.

The next section of the book builds on this understanding. We will explore the reason why this approach is so important by addressing the reason why we are in business in the first place—the consumer. I am going to teach you how to apply your new knowledge to the consumer and use this to succeed in your career.

SECTION TWO
THE CONSUMER: YOUR ULTIMATE BOSS

There is only one boss. The customer. And he can fire everybody in the company from the chairman on down, simply by spending his money somewhere else.

—*Sam Walton, Founder of Walmart*

Everyone Forgets Who Is Really in Charge

As a new manager, who is your boss? The easy answer of course is your direct report—that person who signs your paycheck or gives you a raise at the end of the year. But that is not the correct answer. Although the person to whom you directly report does have a very important influence on your life at your company, the real boss is the consumer. The consumer is the person who actually ends up with your product in the marketplace, whether a product is a piece of mozzarella cheese, a toaster oven, a car, or a service such as insurance—it doesn't matter. The consumer is the ultimate end-user of your product or service.

You can only sell to consumers if they value your product more than the money they possess. A sale is a voluntary trade of value—and money is simply a way of storing value until you are ready to trade it for something you want. Before money, everything was done by barter, directly trading one thing for another or performing a task in exchange for something. Money makes life a lot easier in that respect.

So, the consumer makes a determination if a trade is in their best interest. It takes an incredible amount of effort in most cases to reach that point. Entire marketing and sales teams at companies work to make sure consumers understand the value proposition your company is putting forward. The value proposition is the argument for a trade.

THE ECONOMIC ENGINE DRIVING THE WORLD

This is the amazing thing known as capitalism—using money to facilitate a trade between what you produced for what another has produced. If it is found to be mutually beneficial to both parties, a trade is made. If you want a new 1080p flat screen TV more than the money in your back pocket, you trade. The manufacturer gets your money, and you get the TV. It is a win-win for both parties. Both sides go on their way happy with the outcome.

If one side is not interested in the trade, no feelings are hurt. It is simply not the right match for what the consumer is looking for. A great deal of effort is put into finding out what is of value, and every year we see a parade of new and awesome products hit the marketplace, competing with each other to trade value for value with us. Amazing and beautiful.

Even when people think they are protesting capitalism in front of Wall Street, they are using all of the benefits of capitalism to do so—the planes that brought them there, the taxis that drove them down from the airport, the clothes and the iPhones they wear and use at the event. Even the poster boards and markers from the local craft store were supplied to them by the beauty of capitalism.

Who do these anti-capitalists think sold them the Guy Fawkes masks?

Any type of improvement in the quality of life we experience anywhere in the world was brought to us by the act of two individuals freely trading amongst themselves.
If you want to interact in the world, you must face the inescapable fact that the other half of your partner in this trading process is the consumer. You may not see them face to face, but you need to recognize this before you can begin to understand how you impact the world.

THE CONSUMER IS YOUR BOSS

So, from this perspective , the consumer is your boss. Hopefully this is crystal clear by now. *Consumers are not in the office, so how does this actually impact you?* They are not there, but they need to be in your mind. The consumer is the person you need to take into consideration when you are doing your job. You need to link what you do to their desires. If you cannot, why are you there? Your boss at your company is most likely considering this from the consumer's perspective, so you need to figure it out, and fast.

EXAMPLES TO HELP CLARIFY YOUR ROLE IN RELATION TO THE CONSUMER

1. **Sales:** It is your job to sit down with the consumer to work out the trade. It may be directly or through another party, such as a grocery store or a car

dealership. You work to agree on a final price that is fair for both sides so the trade can happen.

2. **Marketing**: You work to get the consumer to the table with sales in the first place. Why should consumers buy this product? What value does it provide, and why should they spend their money on this?

3. **Research and Development**: This department helps to make the vision of the consumer a reality. The marketing group helps provide direction on what the consumer is saying, and R&D helps to make this vision an actual product or service.

4. **Customer Service**: You actually talk to customers, helping them order what they want and getting it to them when they want it. You also answer questions and help with problems.

5. **Manufacturing**: They take the product R&D creates in the lab and make it real for the world in a production environment, replicating it efficiently so the price is something appealing to the consumer.

6. **Finance and Accounting**: They keep track of the money so the company has the necessary resources to produce and grow. They provide the gas the company machine requires to operate.

7. **Quality**: They are the soul of the company that makes sure the manufactured product is what the consumer expected in the first place. They make sure the company delivers what it promised.

8. **Executive Leadership**: They provide the long-term vision and planning for the company to ensure the value proposition and purpose remain clear over the long run. In other words, what will the consumer want five to ten years from now?

You get the idea. The problem is we can easily get lost in the weeds. It is very easy to forget why we work for a company. This also applies to contractors or entrepreneurs, who have to wear all or most of the hats at any given time. This is a greater challenge, but the expectations are the same.

THE STANDARD OF THE GOOD

This relationship to the consumer is what I refer to as the "Standard of the Good." This is the measurement we all need to consider when doing our jobs, and it is why I argue that the consumer is the ultimate boss. You work for a supervisor who has a great deal of impact on your job satisfaction, but if your company forgets the consumer, it is only a matter of time before the company goes bankrupt and is tossed into the bin of failed companies.

Management Mini-Lesson: First-rate managers and companies never lose sight of their real boss—the consumer.

Did you know Kodak invented the digital camera? Way back in 1975, an engineer named Steve Sasson invented the first digital camera. His bosses were not impressed. By the time Kodak realized what they had, it was too late. Even the money they made off of the patents was not enough to keep the company from filing for bankruptcy in 2012. They weren't able to foresee the consumer's future needs, and they paid the price for their blindness.

WHAT IS QUALITY?

Quality is simply what the consumer expects. It is the expectation that lives in the consumer's mind. It is the understanding of what drives the transaction between the company selling a product and the consumer who wants it. If you buy an Oreo cookie, you know in advance *exactly* what to expect. You know the color of the cookie, how to open the package, what the logo stamped in the cookie looks like, and so on. This is the identity of the Oreo.

If any of these things are below expectations, you are not happy. If they are severely below, you will call or email a complaint to the company. If the issue continues, you may stop buying the product altogether.

Consider why *store* brands do so well. Did you know they have an ever-growing percentage of a grocery store's business? They get more and more market share every year. As a consumer, you perform an experiment every time you consider a purchase based on value. When you buy the store brand imitation Oreos instead of real Oreos, you are performing a comparison between the imitation and your mental standards for the original.

If the store version of the Oreo cookie is close enough to the real one and no real difference in your perception of the cookie is there, then your decision comes down to price. If the store brand is close enough, you buy it, instead of the real thing. Oreo loses market share as a result. If the store brand is successful enough, it may actually force Oreo to lower its price in order to sway your decision in its favor.

WHAT DESTROYS QUALITY?

Products are killed in small steps. It happens when quality is not preserved and corners are cut. It never happens all at once. It is done slowly over time. Companies are not static, and the people who made the changes left the company a long time ago. No one remembers who did what and why.

Often the new person who comes into the company doesn't have the same background in quality assurance. No one sees damage done to the brand identity over time. But once the brand identity line is crossed, consumers will lose trust and stop buying.

THAT FEELING ON THE SWING—AN EXAMPLE

Let's say you work in the research and development department for a small company that makes ice cream in upstate Vermont. It's a premium product, with tons of flavor. The ice cream is hand-churned using milk and cream from local organic farms whose cows feed in green pastures all summer long. The texture is perfect and full of your favorite ingredients.

Huge chunks of real Belgian chocolate sit on your spoon and melt perfectly with the ice cream as you eat. The caramel that's swirled in is the perfect balance of sweet and salty. You labored over this formula for years to get it just right. You sit on your back porch in a swing, eating this after a long day in the office, as you watch the sunset. This is the type of treat that makes life worth living. You love what you do, and it brings pleasure to thousands of people just like you every day.

Hungry? Got your wallet out yet? This is value. It is why a consumer will trade his hard-earned money for your ice cream. The money spent was far less than the pleasure received from eating this ice cream. Consumers will tell friends at work all about this awesome ice cream. They will take pictures to display on Facebook or Instagram. The consumer appreciates the product and what it provides, and will continue to buy it as an occasional treat. Word gets out, and more and more people buy this fantastic ice cream.

THE CRITICAL DECISION

Now, let's say that in your job at R&D, you are sitting at your desk one day minding your own business. The boss comes in for a discussion. The look on her face lets you know it's not going to be a fun one.

"Listen, John," she begins, "I was just up with the accounting team, and we have some serious financial issues with the formulation of the product. We need to take some cost out of the ice cream. The price of chocolate has skyrocketed, and the product is too expensive to make now. We are losing money on every pint we make. Fix it, now!" she delivers.

This one-way conversation sets the stage. You get to work on the formula, trying to figure out ways to make the product cheaper. You look at all the ingredients and find out the chocolate really *is* driving up the cost. You bring in the procurement team to help, and you explain the situation. You look at samples of chocolate from other companies to see if a cheaper version that is the same can be found. You run trials, and product is evaluated.

Finally, you sit down with your boss and present your work.

The boss tastes the ice cream and declares it is "close enough." She decides this while looking at how much money the change in chocolate will save the company. She smiles at you, and you leave the room. You are not smiling. You know it is not even close to the same. Quality is being reduced to save cost.

The same scenario comes up again over time, and the same process is repeated. Maybe less chocolate is added, maybe the cream level is changed, maybe the line speed is increased to get out more pints in an hour. The profitability of the product is fantastic, and everyone appears to be happy.

The consumer buys the product in the grocery store after

a hard day's work. His porch looks inviting as the sun sets. "Another perfect day in paradise. I haven't had this ice cream in quite a while, but I deserve it," the consumer thinks as his spoon carves out a dollop from the top.

The first bite hits his tongue. Instead of smiling, he feels confused. The ice cream is not as smooth as he remembers. The chocolate is hard and does not melt as it should. The caramel is grainy and has a funny aftertaste.

He picks up the carton and scowls. "This shit is not what I want," he mutters, throwing it in the trash.

Sales drop, more cost-cutting measures are put in place, and the product is eventually removed from the grocery store shelves for lack of sales. Marketing campaigns are tried, and sales are pushed to bring in more business, but the product has changed and the consumer has moved on.

Quality is brought in to "fix" the product—but even that does not work.

The bottom line is that no one in the company is sure what happened, and the consumer is not likely to tell you. He just moves on to a product that gives him that feeling he had on the porch—and it's no longer you.

TRUST

The trust you create with the consumer is very fragile. Before the Internet, feedback from the consumer was very hard to get. Focus groups would be brought in for market studies; test markets were set up in areas of the country as were all kinds of advertising and promotions to get consumers to try a new product. Those practices are all still in place, but the cycle of feedback is much, much faster now.

If consumers are displeased, they take pictures and post them on Instagram or on the company Facebook page. You know right away when you screw up the value proposition and so does everyone else. If you really make consumers mad, they may even start a blog and use it to beat you over the head every day. Ouch.

Trust is the consumer's conviction that what you provide will remain the same over time.

> Management Mini-Lesson: If you make a product "better," then you need a conversation to let consumers know what you did.

We all know the phrase "new and improved"—and too often the changed product is neither.

THE GOLDEN RULE OF CONSUMER SATISFACTION: CONSUMERS COMPLAIN WHEN SOMETHING IS DIFFERENT.

It may be better, it may have a sweeter taste, it does not matter. You changed it, and in most cases that really ticks people off. Marketing cases litter the halls of academia with stories of companies who thought they understood what consumers wanted, changed a product, and got their butts kicked around until they changed it back. You can only survive this if you are a big company with vast resources. Even so, consumers will remind you of your failure for as long as they live.

For your case study reading enjoyment, I present—New Coke . . . a blunder from way back in 1985. This is a textbook story of what can wrong if you don't understand what you are messing with.

Coke took an iconic brand and tried to change it for a

really bad reason. They thought people wanted Pepsi's flavor profile, so they tried to match it. What were they thinking? No amount of marketing can win people over when they are attached to a different product profile. More importantly, why did they try? Their data was flawed.

This happened over 30 years ago, yet it still serves as a test case in what not to do when you manage a brand. It was an incredible blunder and one where consumers voted very quickly with their dollars. Coke is not Pepsi. If you want to read more, a link to a Wikipedia story is in the reference material.

> Management Mini-Lesson: Never forget who the boss is. They like what you make and woe to anyone who tries to mess with that.

The Ultimate Loss of Trust—A Recall

A recall is when you breach the trust of the consumer and need to remove product from the marketplace. It is an admission that you let out product that should never have seen the light of day. Companies go out of business in the blink of an eye when this happens.

A recall breaks the trust around a product concerning food quality or safety. It is the one thing every person who walks in my shoes dreads. We work very hard to keep a recall from happening, knowing that in the worst cases, people could die. No one wants that on their conscience.

A recall is a public admission that you are not very good at running your business—or worse.

What Is a Complaint?

What exactly is a complaint? We see them all the time—we stand in line at McDonald's and see someone yelling at the young kid behind the counter. They are mad as hell that they asked for no ketchup on their cheeseburger, but there it is! How can anyone mess up something so simple?

In situations like this, I don't feel sorry for the customer. I feel sorry for the cashier. More than likely it is their first job, their first venture into the world of work. The error was more than likely not their fault; it was another young person behind the order station who wasn't paying attention to the order and just put a regular burger into the box. As long as they did it efficiently, right?

It is interesting how most people in these situations project the actions of the entire organization onto the person in front of them. They know this person did not actually make the burger, yet they assign the blame to them personally, as if they did.

For anyone who works in customer service, they see this phenomenon every day when dealing with the public. They are regarded as the person at fault for the error or issue that was found.

This ties into an important concept in how people view a company—they view it as a single entity, as an individual who as let them down, not as a team of people who are working within a process to complete a task. As a manager, knowing this is key.

Notice too, when the manager is called over at the restaurant, they are suddenly NOT viewed as part of the issue. The angry customer knows the manager did not make the burger, but rather manages the worker who did. The customer deals with the manager as if they were on the same side of the problem.

"Good, a manager, fix this!" they yell at the manager.

"Ma'am, we will do our best to find the issue. Now, what seems to be the problem?" responds the manager in the most impartial tone possible.

"This idiot put ketchup on my burger when I explicitly asked for no ketchup."

"Okay, I can fix this for you. What would you like me to do?" asks the manager.

The customer responds in a lower tone, "I would just like my money back. I'm not hungry any longer . . ."

"Absolutely, and we are sorry to have inconvenienced you. I will get that for you immediately," offers the manager.

"Thank you, that is all I wanted" is the reply, and, by this point, the customer is becoming aware of the scene they caused and most likely feels a little embarrassed.

Was the manager somehow in a position to fix this issue more than the cashier? No, not really. The consumer just wanted to have someone outside of the conflict and in a position of authority resolve the matter. Even though they both work for the same company, the manager is viewed as impartial by the consumer.

Management Mini-Lesson: A dissatisfied consumer typically views a business as a single entity that has let them down. They typically don't see the reality of the situation—that it is a team of people who are working within a process to complete a task. However, the dissatisfied consumer typically views the manager as impartial and on their side. This places the manager in a great position to resolve the situation.

COMPLAINT ESCALATION

This interaction happens all the time. The problem today is that people can vent about their problems online, without the benefit of bringing in a manager for resolution. In social media, people vent their complaints. Pictures are posted on Facebook pages for businesses, and complaints are registered. The person at the company who is responsible for responding will reply for the company and issue an apology.

This is the same as the first scenario; however, if this resolution is unsatisfactory, there is no way for the customer to escalate the complaint. No manager is around to call to the front of the store. Plus, you no longer have just a couple of people in line who are listening—you have everyone who is on that internet page looking over your shoulder.

Companies need a way to bring an issue to the attention of a manager, someone, in this case, who is viewed as an authority who can quickly and easily resolve the issue and is perceived as on the side of the customer. Does any social media site do this? Not that I have found. And they should.

Now, if you work for a company that is known for championing causes and the customer has a vested interested in said cause, the issue is now amplified. A perceived slight may even result in the birth of a blog just to beat you over the head with your failure for years to come.

"Okay, this is great, but how does this impact me as a new manager?" you may be thinking. If you forgot, look at the beginning of this section again. The customer is the one who is really in charge--nothing happens unless the customer gives us money for a burger.

THE COMPLAINT BUCKETS

Complaints fall into two main buckets:
Bucket One: Safety-Related Complaints

These are complaints that the product jeopardizes the health or safety of the consumer. These are obviously very serious and need to be handled immediately. Product recall happens in this category.

Examples include:

- Ice cream containing *Salmonella*
- Toys from China containing paint with lead
- Dog food with dangerous chemicals in it
- A car with defective airbags

Bucket Two: Quality-Related Complaints

These are the rest of the complaints. They are complaints where the value proposition of the item is not as expected.

Examples here include:

- Your bread had mold on it when you bought it.
- You bought a carton of eggs and one was missing.
- Your radio in the new car you just bought doesn't work.
- You ordered a mushroom pizza, but they forgot the mushrooms. I hate that.

Responses to complaints fall into two categories. Safety-related complaints, when detected, are immediately sent up the chain of command in companies. They are usually found when a consumer lets the company know what is going on, e.g., a reported illness or something similar. They can also be detected by a government agency doing testing or by the company itself when performing quality checks on the product. Doctors can also report illnesses to the company or to a government agency.

When a food safety issue is identified, an emergency team is activated to investigate the issue. Potentially, things in this area are hard to detect or complex in nature. The important first reaction of a company should be to gather the facts and the data to evaluate the risk (i.e., ground itself in reality). Yes, a consumer may have become sick from the ice cream. Is food poisoning verified? Did a doctor make the diagnosis? Symptoms from *Salmonella* can take a while to show up. People tend to blame their illness on the last thing they ate, but this is usually not the case.

Could this illness have originated with another food the consumer ate? These questions are important so a company can decide with the best available data at the time. More data or information may become available later, but sometimes you can't wait.

Management Mini-Lesson: When a safety situation happens, you need to make a decision quickly, based on the best available information you have at the time.

If you wait too long to decide, you are simply putting people at risk, and no company wants to do that. If you react too soon and the cause is actually something else, you can scare the public for no reason. Either way, trust is severely damaged.

If a food quality issue happens, the information goes to the quality assurance department. They take the data and begin an investigation. Where was the product made? Most items have a lot code that tells the company all kinds of information—what plant made it, what day it was made, even what line it was made on. When you look at the documentation for that day, you can determine what shift and who was working. You can learn a lot about that production run.

The goal of the quality team is to find out what went wrong. Was it something that happened in the plant? A surprising amount of the time, it is not. It is important to store product at the right temperature, and even in the right location, once it is purchased. Did you know the temperature on the inside door of your fridge is much warmer than in the back? If you keep your milk on the door, it will spoil much faster. Milk contains living bacteria that grows faster in a warm environment. This can result in a complaint that the company can resolve, simply by using better communication about product handling and how the consumer needs to care for the product.

This brings up an important point. Both sides of the transaction need to keep up their ends of the bargain to maintain the product. If you never change the oil in your car and the engine seizes up, whose fault is that? A complaint to the company will not go very far. Certain facts of reality need to be understood and complied with.

Have you ever seen written on a package of food, "Please use within 5–7 days after opening"? Ever wonder where that timeframe came from? This is the time it will take mold to grow once you open the package and spores land on the product. Once the package is open, the countdown commences. The company can neither go and sterilize the air in your home, nor would you want them to.

Management Mini-Lesson: Reality is the judge in these scenarios, and as a manager, you need to take this into consideration when you are working in your role. As we discussed in the first section, reality is what it is, and when something goes off the rails, you need to look at reality to find the answer.

The important activity is to re-establish the consumer's trust. Rational people understand that mistakes happen; they want to know why an issue happened and what you are doing about it.

THE TYLENOL CASE STUDY

In the Chicago market in the early 80s, a person with evil intent placed altered bottles of Tylenol on the shelves of stores. These bottles contained cyanide-laced capsules. Seven people died as a result of this horrible and senseless crime.

Tylenol, a subsidiary of Johnson & Johnson, reacted by removing all product from the shelves in the entire metro area and began a public communication campaign to let people know what was going on.

Tylenol did such a good job of explaining the situation that the public understood they were just as much a victim of this madman as the public was. Most importantly, the public saw Johnson & Johnson put the welfare of its customers over the value of its product. Actions were put in place to prevent a reoccurrence, and things returned to normal. Have you ever wondered where the widespread use of tamper-resistant packaging came from? Now you know. More information is in the reference material at the end of the book.

> Management Mini-Lesson: Trust is easily lost and is exceptionally hard to regain.

WHAT DO WE NEED TO MAKE?

An important aspect that has not yet been discussed is— *what do you actually make? How do you determine what the consumer wants and then meet that need?* The need to find answers to these questions is why you have the job you are in. We are all trying to find the best products the consumer is interested in buying.

What Does the Consumer Want?

That is the million-dollar question. It is hard to find an answer, and the answer never stays the same. It changes and morphs. Organic, low fat, good gas mileage, the list goes on and on. What is interesting is that the consumer may not know the answer either.

How do you find out?

You have two main tracks you can pursue:

1. Evaluate existing product feedback
2. Attempt new product innovation

The tactics you take for the two categories can be, and usually are, very different.

Existing Product Feedback

This is where you take a product that is already out in the market to see if it can be "better."

Better can mean a variety of things:

1. Quality improvement to reduce complaints
2. Cost reduction to improve margin
3. Size change to entice new customers
4. Formulation changes to improve performance
5. Shelf-life extension to reduce losses from expired on-the-shelf product

These are just a few examples of the many different ways a product can be modified based on consumer feedback.

If you have a brand or an existing product that is well-known, this can be very dangerous water (see previous Coke® example) and you can end up alienating your customer base. This alienation can be exacerbated if you have additional certifications or value-added messaging on the package or linked to the product.

An example of this would be organic products. If you make a 100% organic product, and you decide to remove the certification from the product because it is too expensive to make based on the ingredients, you are in for a rough ride.

People buy organic products for a variety of reasons, one of which is a perception of higher quality and food safety. I am not here to tell you if it is true or not—that is not the point. Consumers purchase the products for those reasons. Once they find out you have changed a certification, you may lose them forever.

Most companies will undertake market research before they make a major change to a product or even a service. They will hire an agency or bring in a focus group of consumers to gather information. Different versions of the change are presented, and feedback is analyzed to see if the change is a positive enhancement or not.

If the change is significant enough, companies may test the change in a limited market in the field to see how it compares to the standard product. These types of systematic approaches can be very valuable in improving or changing a product. It pays to be very careful in these situations.

New Product Innovation

This is what research and development scientists live for. They get to figure out how to make a brand-new product. No one has done it before, and they are itching to figure out how to do it. Maybe they get their names on a patent and change the world. Unfortunately, that rarely happens.

When you delve into producing a new product or service that no one has seen before, you are in dangerous territory. The direct feedback you get based on an existing product goes out the window. You have a track record with your existing product, a real-world benchmark that can tell you if it's better or worse. It's kind of like your experience at the eye doctor.

"Which one is better when you look at the chart? One or two . . . *click* . . . One or two?" You can dial in on the expectation based on the previous example. It is a direct comparison with what you know.

A new product has no such reference. To make matters worse, the focus panel members have no reference either. They can only try and compare the new product to something else in their minds that may be similar, but in reality may not be what the researcher is after. Plus, people in these situations tend to give answers they THINK you want to hear.

For example, if you ask someone if they are healthy and exercise 5 days a week for 30-minutes, they are going to say yes. Do they actually do it? Most likely not. Do they only buy healthy, organic produce from single-sourced farms high in the Andes mountains? Of course they do; only the best will do for their little tykes. They are lying, and if you believe them, you are in for a spectacular product launch failure. People tend to avoid what they perceive may be a confrontation.

The easiest way to see if they really do want to buy an item is to ask them to put their money where their mouth is.

"Great!" you share with them. "At the end of the focus group, you have the special opportunity to purchase the products you are tasting today." Will they actually pay three times as much for the spinach that is single source, traceable-to-the-farm organic? Maybe, but most likely not. Money talks.

The key to stand-out market innovation is to produce items the public is not even aware it wants. Steve Jobs got this one right.

> *It's really hard to design products by focus groups. A lot of times, people don't know what they want until you show it to them.*
>
> —*Steve Jobs, Businessweek, May 25, 1998*

Management Mini-Lesson: New product innovation is sexy, but it should only be a minor part of your activity. Most of the actions of your team should be focused on improving the products you already have. This will create the easiest return on investment for your research budget dollar.

THE BEST TOOL I HAVE EVER FOUND TO IMPROVE PRODUCTS

Early on in my career, I found myself in the role of quality director for a major food company's North American division. This was a top role, and I reported to the operations team's vice president. An interesting thing happens when you step up to this level of responsibility—you are alone. No one is there to show you what to do, so you have to figure it out for yourself.

Luckily, I had some mentorship on a key program from

one of the leaders of quality in Europe. He taught me a very important lesson about how to measure customer satisfaction. He took three days to explain how it worked and, more importantly, why it worked.

I am going to share it with you here. If you want to drive product improvement in your company, this is how to do it.

We had a quality questionnaire that went in the product. (My example is based on the technology at the time; you can update this for the Internet by putting in a unique code for entry on a website but it must be linked to a specific product and code date of manufacture.)

It works like this:

The consumer opens the package. It could be cheese, it could be bread, or it could be a product that is more complicated—the options are only limited by your creativity. My example is from cheese. The survey was inside a small plastic pouch to keep it dry and separate from the product. Food safety always needs to be maintained.

The questionnaire was not included in all production runs. We would include it in a run every other month or so; it all depended on how much feedback we needed. If the product was liked and the volume growing, then we would need fewer surveys. If quality issues were present or sales were down, we would add more.

The survey itself dealt only with quality questions. This was very important. No marketing information was asked for. We would gather a consumer's contact information, so we could send a coupon to cover their time for the survey.

Even that amount was carefully calculated because we only wanted people who were more interested in helping us improve the product than receiving something in return.

The survey questions followed this pattern:

Contact information for the consumer.

Date that the product was first opened.

Code date on the bottom of the package.

Specific questions around quality attributes that stayed the same:

- appearance
- texture
- taste
- flavor

These questions were carefully worded and gave the consumer a "Goldilocks Choice" for a response:

- *too hot*
- *just right*
- *too cold*

Example:

Did you find the flavor of the cheese . . . ?

Too salty   Just right amount of salt   Not salty enough

These choices would allow us to hone in on the specific attributes of cheese.

Then we would ask them to grade the product on a five-point scale:

1. *fantastic*
2. *wonderful*
3. *as expected*
4. *disappointing*
5. *terrible*

Finally, there was a section to fill in comments if they chose to.

That's it, but like most things that are elegant, it was focused and extremely well considered.

As the quality director, I could then take the data and figure out some key measures. This made for a kick-butt report everyone in the company loved to look at and analyze.

1. *Average product age from manufacture at which the consumer was buying the product*

   This allowed me to know how long it takes the product to reach the store and how long it actually sits there.

2. *A comparison of product from the same code date*

   I could see if consumers rated it the same when the variables were similar or if age made a difference.

3. *Key defects for the product*

   When a consumer marked down a defect (too salty), what score did they give it? Did they mark it down lower than other defects? How did this impact the overall score for the product?

4. *Overall score*

   This was where the rubber met the road. The score gave me their overall impression of the product at a given age.

5. *Comments*

   This was helpful to see what consumers were thinking and to understand why they praised or punished my product. We would attach these to the reports so people inside the company could hear directly from the consumer about the product.

TYING IT ALL TOGETHER

Now I had a tool that could tell me at what point a product score dropped in the market and what the leading defects were for that product. This gave R&D the information it needed to improve the product based on actual data from the field. I also knew what the impact would be if we wanted to change anything.

For example, if the sales group wanted to increase the shelf life of the product to reduce losses on the shelf from expired products being thrown away, I could show them this graph.

It shows that if we increase our shelf life by five days from 55 to 60 days, the "liking" score of the product will drop like a stone. You may think you are saving money by reducing waste, but what you are doing is chasing away customers, reducing product velocity, and making the problem worse.

The correct answer is to work on the perceived consumer defects to increase sales and leave the shelf life alone.

PRODUCT STORE SURVEYS

Another great method for seeing how your product is performing is to gather product from the marketplace. You want to gather actual product from the field so you can see how it is handled in the supply chain. A lot of damage, for instance, can take place when kids (or even adults . . .) handle the merchandise in the back of the grocery store. From that, temperature abuse of the product can easily occur. Often processes far down the supply chain can cause issues you are completely unaware of.

You can hire companies to pull samples for you, or you can ask your sales group to go to stores and pull them for you. Either way, set up a viewing of the samples so everyone who is interested can take a look. Make sure this is a learning environment and not one people use to beat up other groups over quality. Use this method sparingly, as it is expensive and can test the patience of your sales team members if they are asked to pull samples too often.

DESIGN CONTROL

What is design control? This is the process of changing or creating new products. We now know the most important question in this process is *What do our consumers want?* Based on what you have learned so far, it can be difficult to tell. Changes to existing products are the safest bet, but that does not usually bring in new customers. If you never develop new products, then you are just selling to the same people you sell to now. You can use expensive marketing on TV or the Internet, but the cost is often beyond the means of most companies.

If you choose to innovate and create new products, it is a long process with an outcome that is usually unsure. It is a little like a bet in a casino. You can do research to try and reduce the odds of failure, but it is still a gamble. Companies need to take this risk, but you can really only put a few of your eggs in this basket. If you swing for the fences at every at bat, you are going to sit on the bench most of the time.

This brings us to what is referred to in manufacturing as

design control. This is the overall process of selecting what you work on for product development in research and development. It is the single biggest challenge any company can undertake, and it decides the future of the organization.

This is what it looks like:

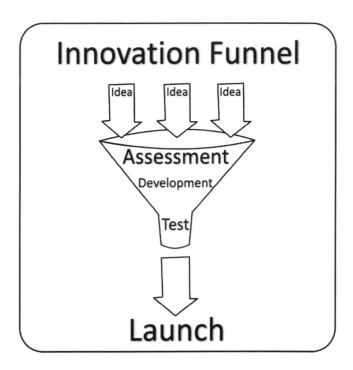

If you work in marketing, this looks familiar. It is the funnel diagram used to show how customers are brought into a campaign and sold on a product.

How It Works

You have ideas at the top--the more the better, and they can really come from anywhere. Ideas for the two main categories (new and existing products?) are brought to the team for review. This is after some initial vetting to determine if they are remotely feasible. If an idea is remotely feasible, then a committee is the next step. This group has the job of looking at the initial project to determine if it meets the criteria for moving further along in the process. Criteria can include things like:

1. Cost reduction
2. Quality improvement
3. Line extension
4. Product requested by a customer (Walmart, Target, etc.)
5. Packaging change
6. New product

The committee then looks at the merits of the project to determine if it is something the organization should work on. The challenge for the committee is to pick out only the ideas that make the most sense for the business. The first pass is always profitability; if the product is too expensive to make versus the price you can charge, it is killed off as an idea immediately.

Friction can develop when ideas are not moved forward. People submit ideas because they have a need. If you work in sales, your retailers want complete sets of products for a display or multiple sizes to satisfy their need to fill space and have sufficient products to sell. This interest does not usually match up with those of the organization, yet efforts are made to move the project into the funnel based on the relationship with the customer. These types of projects can be dangerous and need to be approached with caution.

The innovation funnel? The committee vetting? Process is very important for a company. You will always have more projects than you can do and an overly ambitious idea of how many things your people can work on at any given time. The result is that projects are rushed and corners are cut to meet launch dates. Shelf-life studies that should be run are not. Consumer feedback trials are limited in scope and are not long enough. Ingredient stability testing is put off for a later date and so on. Each of these things is a risk, and the company is assuming everything will go perfectly. It usually does not. A process of deciding the right thing to do, with the right people will help prevent these from happening.

The other big mistake is timing. Once a project is selected, the timing is usually based not on how long it will take to do it, but on when the company wants to launch it. Customers such as Target have set periods where they perform what is known as a "shelf reset." The buyers for a company will take a look at all the items they sell. They know which ones are good and which ones are not making money. They look to replace these with ones that are better. They look to companies to make the products that are going to fill these empty slots on their shelves, and this is normally only done at certain times during the year.

This time is then used as the deadline to have the product developed. If it is January and the customer does a reset in November, this is the deadline to get the product completed and on the store shelf. It fails to consider any of the complexities of the project or if it is realistic. The response of the company is to push those on the project team to meet the deadline, so corners are usually cut to do so. This increases the risk of a mistake or more serious issue with the product failing in some way. It could be in terms of quality or shelf life or some other unknown.

Management Mini-Lesson: Be wary of rushing the development of a new product and ignoring important, related support processes in order to meet a launch date set by outside buyers.

PROJECT RESOURCE PIPELINE

The other side of the project coin is resources. No matter how big a company is, you only have so many people available to work on a project and so much to time get it done. Your team of 10 can work 20 hours a day, but it still only adds up to 200 available man hours. No more hours exist. Plus, that assumes they are only working on this one project, but in reality they are working on multiple projects at once. Now throw in travel time if the plant location is remote, and you lose even more time. You always end up doing less than you think you can in theory.

The problem in most cases is the team that selects projects is not the team who actually does the projects, so you have a disconnect on what can get done and in what timeframe.

Like most things in life, it all depends on how many people can work on something and how much time you have to get it done.

What is the solution to this dilemma? It is a common one and something companies need to address. The people side is static (it's hard to hire people), so the other side of the coin needs to be looked at—time.

You know the schedule of when your customers are going

to ask for new products. It happens the same time every year. Build out a pipeline over multiple years. You can plan out further ahead, and not just research products for this year, target 18 months out for a presentation to the customer at that time. Then you can look at your available resources in the company and the time you have to work on it.

You then slot in product improvement projects, cost reduction initiatives, ingredient changes, and all the other projects that need to get done as well. Smart companies will leave a little wiggle room for surprise projects or changes which need to be done quickly. For example, a supplier of an ingredient goes out of business and an alternate needs to be found to keep production running. These types of emergencies happen all the time (remember what happened with the whey production I described earlier in the book?).

Management Mini-Lesson: Exemplar management doesn't get caught in the day-to-day processes. Instead you develop out your pipeline, planning further ahead for years to come.

This approach works, but companies have a very hard time getting out of the hamster wheel to start the process. They are caught in the day-to-day process and can't get it to the stage where they need to develop out the pipeline. This requires discipline at the senior level to put off some larger projects to allow for timeline development. Never easy.

I hope you are starting to see just how important the consumer is to your company. You may work in finance or quality as a new manager—it doesn't matter. The consumer is critical to how we run our business and is the voice that needs to be consulted at every turn:

- New product development
- Changes to existing product
- The value proposition and why consumers buy from you
- What criteria they use to judge your product
- The trust between consumer and company
- How complaints are evaluated and responded to
- If it goes off the rails, how to manage a recall to minimize damage

Hopefully you are noticing a theme with what I have been talking about so far. This gets back to what we discussed in the first section and why this is so important—

Reality is king.

It is our job to figure out what is going on in the real world and translate it to our work. What do consumers really want? If they are upset, what is the reason why? What do we do about it?

PLAN-DO-CHECK-ACT

An important tool in quality assurance is this simple little diagram:

This is the method of understanding what is going on around you in any situation.

Plan: What do you want to achieve?

Do: Take your plan and execute it.

Check: Did the plan go the way you expected?

Act: Incorporate new findings into the plan and repeat the process.

You need to make sure the consumer is the central point in this process and is always consulted or considered before making a change.

More to come on this later in the book—and how you can apply this to any job you are in charge of.

The other key process we have not yet looked at in detail is the most important one—*how do you make sure the voice of the consumer is heard in the manufacturing plant?* This is a very difficult one for companies to achieve. I have a method I am going to share with you in the next section.

ACTION PLAN: KNOW YOUR CONSUMERS

Your goal now is to find out who your consumers are. The easiest way to do this is to talk with your sales team. At first, they may be suspicious of why you want to do this. After all, how many people ask to do this? Who are you selling to in your company? Arrange to actually talk to some consumers in person. Find out why they buy from you. The more you understand, the better the manager you will be, no matter your position in the company. This is not easy, and some people may be confused about why you want to do this. That's fine, let them be. You know something they don't. Find a way to understand and apply the principles I have advocated in this section, and you will be highly valued in the company.

This is the New Manager Mindset at work. You understand the mechanisms that allow your company to meet the objectives of your boss—the consumer. You see the big picture.

CONCLUSION

In summary—consumers are the key to your success. They are the gold standard that needs to be referenced and are often forgotten in the company. It is simply assumed that consumers will always be there. Many very large companies that were here five years ago are out of business today because they forgot to take care of consumers.

Up Next

In the next section, we tie this all together into the most powerful method for executing this plan I have found in my 20-plus years of investigation into these principles.

SECTION THREE
QUALITY SYSTEMS:
WHAT MAKES YOUR WORLD
GO ROUND

Almost all quality improvement comes via simplification of design, manufacturing . . . layout, processes, and procedures.

—*Tom Peters, business writer and speaker*

YES, YOU'VE ARRIVED— WELCOME TO THE MOST IMPORTANT SECTION OF THIS BOOK

You don't know it yet, but this section is the most important part of the book. This is the area where things begin to make sense and are tied together. Why? Because quality systems are the way businesses work. People are not aware of it because it hasn't been shown to them.

Quality systems are the soul of an organization, it is

how we interact, how we plan, how we measure our progress against a plan and correct course if things are going in a direction that is not good for the plan. This system is the basis for everything that goes on in a company.

Quality systems tell you if things are right or wrong, good or bad, profitable or costly. It is the method we all use, but no one pays attention to its value because it is so ingrained.

Just as with philosophy in the first section, a system of quality is there, whether you are conscious of it or not.

I'm giving you a full picture of quality systems so you can be the most capable manager possible, I will tell you my personal story about how I became acquainted with quality systems. Yes, my story involves certain specifics like bunny suits and cheesemaking, so you might wonder how the systems I'm describing could even apply to you. Do not fear! You will derive the most benefit for your managerial role only by getting acquainted with the big picture, the whole story, and even if my story contains details of sugar water solutions and the FDA—the important takeaways still apply to you. Trust me—I've got your back.

WHAT—GET A REAL JOB?

When I first got out of college, I realized I needed a real job. Funny how those things work. I was living in Laramie, Wyoming at the time, with a fresh, new degree in my hand. I was living at a friend's house and working at a grocery store, stocking shelves at night. I always worked during college. I needed the money to help out, but, more importantly, I wanted to keep busy and do "real-world" activities. I felt college could be too insulating, and, besides, it's nice to have money in your pocket.

Once I realized I needed a 'real' job, I started looking around for one. I quickly found out no one was hiring people with scientific degrees in Wyoming. I didn't want to work at the university, so I widened my net. I found an ad for a substrate technician for a company in the Denver metro area and sent in my rather thin resume, hoping for the best.

I waited for what seemed like an eternity, but one thing was for sure—working the nightshift at the grocery store was not fun. I liked the people I worked with, but the transition between the day and night period of when you were awake on your off days was very difficult. I have a lot of respect to this day for people who do off-shift work .

THE INTERVIEW

I actually got a response to the ad, and an interview appointment was scheduled! I was actually quite surprised and unsure of my next move. The very first move I did know. I drove a dodgy 1979 Datsun B210 station wagon, which was good enough to get me around town, but would most likely not make the trip from Laramie to Denver, a longer than two-hour drive.

Luckily, my roommate's girlfriend, taking pity on me, loaned me her very nice Honda Civic for the trip. Now all I needed were some nice interview clothes and a tie. Oh, and I had to remember how to tie a tie. (My mom had taught me years before but no reasons had come up to wear one in a very long time.)

My interview was on a Monday morning at 9 a.m. sharp. Before I went to bed that night, I watched the weather report, and, of course, it held bad news. A major snowstorm was barrelling down on the entire region, with upwards of 12 inches of snow expected. You have got to be kidding me . . . However, I was young, and it didn't worry me too much. I grew up in Wyoming and knew how to drive in the snow. I would just leave a little earlier to get there on time.

Well, luckily I left a lot earlier. I got up at 3 am and hit the road. It was already snowing hard, and some really tricky driving was in front of me. Laramie, Wyoming sits on top of a high, wind-swept plain at an elevation of 7,165 feet.

The wind always blew there, and now it was howling. A stretch of highway between Laramie and the Colorado border sat in front of me. As soon as you left the city, it was empty and desolate. If you got stuck, you were there for a long time.

I trudged forward, snow already sticking to the roads. It was a white-knuckle experience and one I will never forget. This trip happened 25 years ago as of the writing of this book, and it feels like yesterday.

A drive that normally takes two hours was closer to five and a half. Things got a little easier when I got to Fort Collins but only because the roads were now being plowed. The snow was actually coming down harder as I arrived at the company.

After finding the location, I went to a nearby gas station to change into my interview clothes in the bathroom. I looked at the blankets and provisions I had placed in the back of the Honda in case I got stuck. I was glad I hadn't needed them, so far. I reread my resume, recited some of the answers to questions I expected, and went over to the company.

The interview was at a medical device facility that made identification plates for hospitals. You could take an unknown bacterial sample from a patient, incubate it, and then, based on what substrates the bacteria could use and what it couldn't, you could determine what it was. Pretty slick little product.

The position I was after involved making a lot of those substrates. My potential boss was a very nice lady named Carolyn. We talked, toured the facility, and met with some other folks. Overall, I was pleased with my performance and tried to put on my best face. I thanked them for their time, and we parted ways.

I drove back to Wyoming hoping my world of work was about to begin. Luckily, it was. I got a call from Carolyn who offered me the job, and I readily accepted—exciting! Now, where the hell do I live? Luckily, I had a friend who lived in the Denver area who took pity on me. He rented me a room in the basement of his condo while I found a place of my own. I had no money to pay rent, so I would pay him once I began working. Exciting!

I packed up my belongings and said goodbye to all my friends.. I moved down from Laramie and started a new chapter in my life. It was going to be an important step for me, and I knew it at the time.

My New Life in Colorado

My job was challenging, and luckily I had someone to train me. John was leaving the company but had agreed to stay on and train the new guy. He was a new dad, looking somewhat disheveled most of the time. He and his wife were moving to a new town and a new opportunity for them.

He showed me how to make the substrates and what was expected. Turns out you spend a lot of your day working in a cleanroom. Now, if you have never had the pleasure of working in a cleanroom, you have missed one of the finer pleasures in life.

You work in a room with sterile air. The air is cleaned by banks of filters that remove the bacteria and anything else they can. The rooms are cleaned and scrubbed after every shift to ensure nothing harmful remains in the environment. The product we were making was made to grow bacteria, so if you got contamination from the environment, the product was ruined. If a production run failed, it was tens of thousands of dollars lost to the company.

To work in the cleanroom, you had a whole ritual of how to get ready. The end result was what was known as the "bunny suit." You were covered from head to toe in a white, disposable jumpsuit with a mask, boots, gloves, and glasses. Not fun—the suits were hot and your eye glasses would fog up with every breath. People would come in with particle counters during runs to make sure the air was clean.

You would touch a box of supplies, and the particle counter would go nuts. This was my life now.

John taught me how to do my first real job, and I am grateful to him for this mentorship. In addition to showing me the cleanroom, he introduced me to the world of ISO Quality Standards and Work Instructions. This was to be a turning point for me, learning how things worked in the world of manufacturing.

My First Quality System

First off, what is ISO? The International Organization for Standardization (it's backward because it is European). It is a set of quality standards, a set of rules to follow if you want to make good product. ISO is also a business entity, and you pay them to use their standard. They give you the rules for what systems you need, but not necessarily how to do them. A wide variety of businesses can become ISO certified, such as businesses involving medical devices, food manufacturing, car manufacturing, or any business where you are making a product or even supplying a service. You sign up for the standard, write your programs, and document that you follow them. An auditor comes once a year or so and checks to see that you are following the standard and have records that show you are. The auditor will walk around and talk to people to see if you are really doing what you say.

It's the Plan–Do–Check–Act process again, certified by an outside party. If you pass the audit, a certificate is issued, and you can proudly post it in your office. This shows customers you are a reputable company with good programs in place. At least, that's how it works in theory.

Because the company I worked for is a medical device manufacturer, standards are very high. The Food and Drug Administration oversees the facility, and strict standards are in place. Every production process needs to be documented and validated. Validation means everything needs a plan and calibration programs are in place to measure every action — and I mean everything.

WORK INSTRUCTION HELL

As an example of how detailed the work instructions were, let me give you an example. Here is how you make a 35% sugar solution. These were for use in the identification plates. The process consisted of mixing 350 grams of sugar with 1,000 milliliters of water. Fancy! I would then get dressed up in the bunny suit, go in the cleanroom, and use a sterile filter to remove the bacteria from the sugar water. Let me walk you through the process, so you get the idea.

1. First, you go to the master document book and find the work instruction for the sugar solution you were making and make a copy. You couldn't have them on your computer because you could potentially change the instructions. Then you go to the lab where a person from quality assurance would double-check

to make sure the work instruction you copied was the right one for what you were making.

2. The next step was to make labels with a little label-making machine. It had movable type and you would rotate the dials to get the label information lined up. You would do this based on a master book of labels and what the work instruction said to do. You would print an exact number of labels and put the first and last from the print run in the work instruction to show they were printed. Then, you would go back to the QA lab for a sign off that your labels match the master book and that you printed the correct number of labels.

3. The next step in this list of fun was to gather your supplies. Everything you used in the cleanroom had to be sterile; some items were single-use and were purchased sterile (the filter for the sugar, for example), and the rest had to be sterilized in an autoclave. If you are unfamiliar with an autoclave, it is a chamber you load things in and then, under heated steam and pressure to kill all the bacteria. The items are either sealed in pouches, so they stay sterile, or they have lids to keep out the bacteria. Every load that runs is validated and must be done in an exact sequence. If you need one thing sterilized, you must load everything for that validated load in order to sterilize it.

4. Next up is to get the sugar and weigh it. Well, you would think it is pretty easy, wouldn't you? You simply weigh out 350 grams on a scale after you zero out your container weight, right? Well, kind of. You need to write down the calibration of the scale and the lot number of the sugar into the work instruction. Then you need to go find someone to check that you can indeed weigh out 350 grams of sugar and read the

scale correctly. They initial in the work instruction to verify you did this correctly. You do the same for the water after you measure it in a graduated cylinder.

5. You write down the lot number for the filter and for all the other bits and pieces. Everything goes on a cart, and you then prepare to enter the cleanroom. When you do, you wipe down everything with alcohol to sterilize the outside, then dress up in a bunny suit. Someone goes in the cleanroom with you to monitor the air to make sure no particles are floating around to get in the sugar water.

6. You take samples for sterility testing into the QA lab, and you put the samples in storage for use in a production run at a later date. The last step is to test the filter to make sure it didn't break during the run and was filtering out the bacteria properly.

Congrats, you have just made sterile 35% sugar water. This process took the better part of the morning and is only one small ingredient in the final product.

This was just one simple work instruction out of many I was following to do my job. This was an easy one. In addition, if anything did not go exactly as planned during the process, down to the graph on the autoclave not exactly matching what the book said the run should look like, you had a deviation. That meant you had to go back and document the failure, have someone investigate it to find out why it failed, and then put in corrective actions to prevent it. This would all go in a giant binder with all the things that went wrong. This whole process usually meant more training and more documentation. And I began to dread it.

Is This Really Right?

None of this made any sense to me, so after a few months I asked my boss about it.

"Bryan," she explained, "We are an ISO certified company. This means we follow the programs they say we need and do what the auditors are looking for."

"This may not always make sense, but the FDA looks for these things too," she added.

I countered, "But these are things I was trained to do, and I learned a lot more from John than I ever did from the work instructions."

"Maybe, but that's the way it is," she answered. "It's like this—work instructions need to be written so that anyone can come in off the street, read it, and know how to do a certain task."

"So, my training and college education mean nothing—it's just follow the work instruction, get someone to check that I can read a scale? Doesn't it really mean that I am not even competent to do the most simple task?" I asked.

She looked at me and did not answer.

"What about the person who checks the scale? Doesn't this assume they actually know how to read a scale? Why are they somehow qualified, and I am not?" I continued. "Shouldn't we also have someone who checks the checker?" I asked with a mischievous smile on my face.

"Good question. Just follow the work instruction," she maintained.

The conversation was over.

Really? This is my Life?

That conversation stuck with me because it made absolutely no sense. Was this to be my career? Following ever more complicated work instructions and filling out deviations for the simplest of tasks because I was somehow always judged to be unable to remember how to do it and always in the state of the beginner? Always unable to learn and grow in my knowledge? I didn't like it at all.

That simple lesson was one of the key findings of my career; I just didn't know it at the time.

Management Mini-Lesson: Work instructions are not a replacement for people. You can never write a work instruction that is so detailed that anyone can do a task and never make a mistake. Don't worry, we'll return to this important lesson later in this section to ensure you really grasp it and its implications.

The FDA Drops In for an Audit

While I was at this company, we had a routine audit from the FDA to check our facility, do an inspection, and check our paperwork. The documentation did help, but it was never enough. They were there for two weeks, checking everything and watching us do our work. They looked at the deviations we documented and went over every single one. The result of this audit was good, and no major issues were found in my area, but more documentation would be needed . . . Sheesh.

I decided after the audit that the medical device industry and working in a cleanroom were not for me.

The lessons went with me, and I was grateful for the chance to learn and grow with the people I worked with in bunny suits. Too bad I never got to see what they looked like . . . Just kidding.

THE FOOD INDUSTRY, REVISITED

 As you know from earlier in the book, I found a job working in the food industry as a microbiologist in a lab. This was my next step after the medical device work, and it was more of a direct fit with my college degree. After a grueling interview process, I made the cut and was eager to get started.

My job was as a food microbiologist. I tested the products made at the cheese company to make sure no dangerous pathogens were present—bacteria such as *Salmonella* or other nasty things. The food industry does a great job of making sure the food you eat is safe. Almost all of the time it is, but sometimes failure occurs. My new job was to help prevent failures.

Once I arrived in the lab, the first feature that struck me was the lack of documentation in comparison to medical device manufacturing—no army of people running around with papers and no dedicated validation person checking the autoclave for sterilization in every possible configuration. We also used an autoclave and put test strips in to make sure it worked, but nothing else. It was beautiful.

It was liberating to be able to do my work and not be encumbered by mountains of paper. I worked with another microbiologist who trained me. He taught me how to do the tests like in my last job. He patiently sat me down at the bench and showed me how to plate bacteria and the most efficient way to do it. He then sat back and watched me do it. Just like someone learning to play golf or any new skill, I was slow and awkward. Francis was patient and a good teacher.

This was back when a lot of manual plating was done to test for pathogens. It is more automated now. Back then, the test required putting samples on an agar plate and then letting them grow. If nothing grew, that was what we wanted, but if it did, we had to do additional tests to isolate the bacteria. Good technique helped you do this. The test lot sampled for pathogen testing sat in a warehouse on hold until the testing was done. If it passed, it was released for sale. It if failed, we would sample more to narrow down where the bacteria occurred and what needed to be destroyed. This very rarely happened, which meant the plants were doing a good job of cleaning. This was my first taste of the world of food safety.

Work got done, testing was performed, and the documentation was 10% of what I'd endured in the medical device industry. How could this be? How could work be done and still perform as designed, and I not have to write down every single little action?

I knew the answer—it was the training piece that was more important. The one-on-one activity of sitting down and transferring knowledge was the key. This process can be good or bad, so the trainer needs to do things correctly so bad habits are not passed along. It also needs to be hands-on and not in a classroom. I learned more about plating and how to do it quickly in this way than I ever would have with a work instruction.

> Management Mini-Lesson: Nothing takes the place of one-on-one training—actually sitting down with the person you are training and working with them until they get it.

I filed this away in my mind as a different view of how things actually work in the real world. If I had stayed in medical devices, I would have thought their way was the only way to do it. I would have been wrong.

I worked at this company for almost eight years in

technical and customer support roles. It was a challenging environment and one where I grew significantly in my scope of knowledge. I dealt a lot with customers in my customer support role, and I learned how to interact with them. Sometimes the hard way. Technical knowledge is important, but if you cannot understand the needs of the consumer, you can put in systems that are not necessary. This was how I learned about the importance of the consumer as described in the previous section.

For example, a hamburger contamination issue happened at Jack in the Box in 1993. If you remember, they were undercooking their burgers and people got sick from *E. coli* bacteria. Hundreds of people became ill, and four children died. It was a horrible thing and changed the way the meat industry operated. This case study is well known in the food industry. You will find a link to it in the reference material.

At the time, I was working with a technical group that sold industrial powders for use in food products. This was a byproduct of making cheese and was used in many food items. After the Jack in the Box issue, many customers began calling and asking if we tested for the specific pathogenic organism implicated as the source of the illnesses in the Jack in the Box food safety issue.

We did not. But, we didn't need to. We tested for the family of organisms under which *E. coli* belonged. This was a wider group and covered every type of bacteria in the bacteriological family. If the test was negative for the family, it was negative for all the members of the family, including the *E. coli* in question.

I explained this to our customers and the answer always came back the same, "No, not good enough. We want you to test specifically for *E. coli* to protect us."

This made no sense. It went against everything I knew as a microbiologist, so I asked my boss how to proceed.

"Bryan, everything our customers want can be done for a price," he explained. "Find out from the lab how much the test will cost. We already have to hold it in the warehouse for the other microbiological testing, so let's see."

I did my research and found out that new samples would need to be taken and sent out for testing in the lab. A new method would need to be followed. The cost would be around $250 for every customer request. This was not cheap and would need to be done on every specific lot that a customer wanted the test result for.

I relayed my findings to my boss.

"Good," he responded, "Now relay the cost of the test to the customers and the additional lead time needed to perform the testing. Ask them if they want to proceed and the cost of the test will be added to their invoice."

I told the customers what was required and the additional complexity of the process. I explained again that the test was not necessary and was already covered by any existing test covering the family of organisms under which *E. coli* belonged.

This time my message sank in; no customers wanted us to do the additional testing once they heard the cost. Interesting. Once customers understood the ramifications of their requests in terms of lost time and money, my messaging sank in. Anything can be done for a price, but it doesn't mean you should do it.

> Management Mini-Lesson: The customer can ask for anything, and if they are willing to pay for it, they can have it. Don't accept the irrational at face value. Find a way to bring reality into the conversation.

THE NEXT PHASE OF MY GROWTH

After a little less than eight years with this employer, I made the decision to leave. It was not that I didn't enjoy my work—it was challenging and I liked working with the customers. I left because I wanted to advance and thought it would be easier if I left the company. It was a difficult environment and promotions were few and far between. I learned that if you want to grow, you often have to move. So I did.

I found a job with another food company back East. I began talking with them after a recruiter called me and told me about the position. It sounded really interesting, with a lot of new challenges to tackle. The role was open due to the previous person's promotion into another role, which was also a good thing.

After interviewing, I was quickly offered the job of director of quality assurance. This was a big step and more than a little scary. This was the big chair, and this job was responsible for quality across the entire company, plus a move to the East Coast with my girlfriend. Was I ready for it? The only way to find out was to take the leap. I accepted the job, and we moved.

I was not prepared in any way for my new level of responsibility. Luckily, the previous director was there to train me. Without his help, I would have probably failed. The jump from a role where you are doing things to one of leading people is a big one, and if you are not properly prepared, it can ruin your career.

As luck would have it, the plant where I worked was having its food safety audit the week I arrived on the job. As it turns out, the plant was also ISO certified, just like the company I started with in medical devices.

The ISO standard can be applied to many industries; medical device and food are just two of them. I was to find out the standard itself does not actually ensure the product you make is of good quality and safe; it just documents the process. So, if you have a bad process but you follow it, you can still be ISO certified. Of course, this is a simplification, but you get the idea.

QUALITY IS JOB ONE

A great example of the disconnect between being certified and producing a quality product was an issue that happened between Ford and Firestone Tires. Defective tires were manufactured and were allegedly causing SUVs to roll over. It was estimated that 250 deaths and 300 serious injuries were the result of defective tires that caused the tread to separate from the tire. These tires were mainly made at Firestone's Decatur, Illinois plant.

I remember seeing an executive from Firestone on TV at a press conference in front of the plant at the time of the incident. He was at a podium on the street opposite the entrance to the plant. There was a giant banner over the main entrance directly behind the executive, reading, "ISO 9001 certified." The system was in place, but it obviously did not work. Firestone did a great job of documenting a process that produced flawed tires. Read more on this case study in the reference material at the end of the book.

TRIAL BY FIRE—MY FIRST BIG AUDIT

One of the first things that needed to be done when I arrived at my new job was to ensure the plant would pass the ISO audit. The previous quality director was now the plant manager, so he was able to lend a hand for the audit.

If you have ever worked in quality, audits follow a familiar pattern. You have an opening meeting with the team from the plant in which the auditor explains to everyone what is going on. This means going over the standard, what the auditor is going to look at and with whom the auditor is going to be talking. The auditor thanks the plant for its cooperation in advance. The plant manager then states her commitment to the audit and how happy she is that the auditor is there and that the plant will cooperate in any way needed. Everyone breaks, and the audit begins.

The auditor and the QA manager settle in for what is going to take place over the next few days. They usually set up in a conference room where the QA manager brings a cart that has all the document binders that the plant has in place for its ISO plan. In this case, it was a giant pile of documents. A large cart was rolled into the room with everything on it.

The auditor then gets out his computer and begins to ask questions on the standard and what we need to do to meet it. The QA manager digs into his binders and pulls out documents that were written to address the standard's requirements. Records showing it is was done are reviewed , and the auditor moves on to the next question.

Auditors tend to jump around, not going in a particular order. They ask questions as they think of them, and the QA manager needs to remember where to find the answer to the particular question in his documents. It is not a very efficient system. Plus, you have all your documents there, so it is only a matter of time before the auditor takes the books and starts looking at them directly. This usually generates more questions.

After a while, the auditor gets tired of sitting, so they go out on the floor to see production running. The two may stop by human resources on the way to see employee training records or to understand the hiring process at the company. If you are a food company, you need to follow rules to go out on the plant floor. These are known as "Good Manufacturing Practices," or simply GMPs.

The auditor and QA manager put on protective clothing, hair nets, safety glasses, and gloves. Jewelry and other things that may fall in the product are also removed. They then enter and wash their hands. This needs to take place every time you enter. Out on the floor, the auditor observes what people are doing, looks at records they are filling out, and asks them questions about their jobs. This makes some people very nervous, so it is always interesting to see how it goes. After a while, the two head back up to the conference room.

The auditor takes his notes from the floor and puts them in his computer. All during this process, the QA manager is trying to get an understanding of what the auditor is thinking and if he is going to deduct points from the plant score for anything he has seen.

If the auditor doesn't like something, the QA manager will do his best to explain it to try not to get a point deducted. A lot of times, this is a negotiation because the standard is not always clear on what to do, so the plant will try to explain why they do what they do. They may not win.

Lunch eventually comes, and the two work through it. This cycle continues. After a while, the auditor realizes time is short and a lot of material still needs to be covered. He picks up the pace to finish the audit on time. He asks questions or looks in the documents to find an answer directly. Once he is done, the auditor asks for some time to finish the report, and the QA manager makes one last ditch effort to try to ensure that possible troubling items the auditor finds are not written up as findings in the report.

Once the auditor has completed his findings (this may take a few days, depending on the size of the plant), the management team once again gathers in the conference room for the final report.

The auditor thanks the plant manager for her support and for the excellent cooperation he received from the plant team members. He then dives into the report and goes over his findings. If serious items are found or things are unclear, a lot of discussion can take place. But usually, the audit stays the way it is.

The plant is issued the findings, and they then go about correcting the deviations the auditor found. A final report is issued, and a certificate is placed on the wall. This happens annually at a minimum and also happens for regulatory or customer audits.

Doesn't that sound like fun?

Well, my first big audit did not go too well, and I wasn't sure I was going to have a job by the end of it.

Not Going to End Well

"So," began the auditor, settling in after the opening meeting, "let's dig into the documents, shall we?"

So began the audit, and it went off the rails pretty early. Most of the questions went like this: "I see here in this procedure you have stated a weekly meeting takes place to review the findings of plant inspections. I would like to see the meeting records to show they took place."

"Well," replied the plant manager, "when we wrote that procedure, we wanted to start doing it. We had one kick-off meeting, but we never really got it started. I don't have any records."

"Hmmm" was the reply of the auditor. "I see," he remarked, looking over the top of his reading glasses, "Let's move on to the next question." He scribbled on his notebook.

So went my first audit as QA director. It was a disaster, and the plant barely passed. It wasn't because of the team on the floor; everyone did a great job and answered the auditor's questions. It was because of the documents. They were out of order, things were missing, and records were incomplete or never started.

To make matters worse, the auditor chosen to inspect our food plant had no food experience. What he had was a lifetime of working in the automotive industry. He didn't know anything about making food and wanted us to make cars instead. He had a very hard time translating his knowledge of auto manufacturing to the food industry.

By the end of the carnage, we had accumulated a page and a half of issues with our quality programs at the company. It was not a pretty closing meeting with the auditor. He also took some pity on us and didn't write us up for smaller things he could have put in the report. It was a long drive home that night.

THE AFTERMATH

After the audit, I went back to my office and sat there, unsure of what to do. If this was to be my first job leading quality assurance for a company, it was not off to a good start. Hopefully, they would let me keep my job, so I could figure out what went wrong and fix the mistakes in the system. The next audit was only a year away, and I had to correct all the problems the auditor found before I could begin anything else. I had no idea where to start.

After a day of sitting in my office and avoiding the issue, I decided to dive in and try to figure out what the hell went wrong. My first stop was the plant manager's office. He had written most of the documents and managed the system, so he would hopefully have the answers.

I knocked on his office door. "Hey, Phil," I called and walked into his office. "Got a minute?"

"Sure . . . ," he replied in a tone that said he knew why I was here. He looked like I did after the audit--defeated and unsure.

"What happened?" was my first question. I was not always tactful early in my career.

"Well," he said, "when we wrote the system, we were really under the gun. Corporate told us we needed ISO certification because it was a customer requirement and it needed to be done right away. We only had a few months to get ready, so we had to quickly write the documents needed for the standard. We were going to implement a lot of them, but we forgot and then the auditor found them. What a mess."

"I see . . . please continue," I remarked.

"Most of what the standard says we need to do makes sense; plus I added some things I wanted the plant to do as well," he related. "It's just that we never started."

"A lot of documents were missing during the audit," I commented. "Why is that?"

"Not sure why" was his response. "I thought we had them all, but maybe other people just had them on their computers and forgot about them."

"A lot of the documents were very long," I observed. "Must have taken some serious time to write them."

"Absolutely," he affirmed. "It's important to be clear on the documents as to what we are doing."

Then he said something that hit me like a meteorite on the head. It was a turning point in my career.

"I believe anyone from off the street should be able to take a document from our system, read it, and be able to do a task," he asserted.

I stared at him for what must have been a long time. It was almost WORD FOR WORD what my boss at my first job had said to me about work instructions when I was asking why they were so complicated.

I knew this was important, but I did not know why yet. I was certain about one thing—his was not the right way to go about things. But everyone did it this way! There had to be a better way, and I was convinced I had to find it. I thanked Phil and went back to my office.

Management Mini-Lesson: You can't set up systems that you wish would work. People will continue doing things the way they were trained. You can write as many documents as you want, but until you change the behavior, you are going to fail.

The Beginning of a New System

Staring at my computer, my first task was clear—find all the documents.

This first task was much more difficult than I'd realized. Documents were everywhere! The receptionist had some hard copies, but nothing on her computer. The purchasing department had a lot of good procedures, but they didn't match mine. Theirs were more up-to-date, so I got those. I went out on the floor and found all kinds of documents in the desks of the supervisors.

My next stop was sanitation. The sanitation manager was intelligent and a very hard worker. He worked on the night shift, so the only time I saw him was when I was arriving in the morning and he was going home to sleep. I could catch him and chat for a second to see how things went before he left.

A couple of days previously I had sent him an email asking for his documents. We had some for the audit, but like all the other departments, many were missing.

"Dave, good morning!" I declared as I saw him coming down the stairs from the upstairs offices. "How did it go last night?"

"Not too bad" was his reply. It most likely did not go smoothly. Sanitation is a tough job, and they are always pressured to do it as quickly as possible. When your plant is not running while you are cleaning equipment, you are not making product. So you are not making any money.

"I got your documents, thanks," I told him. "A lot of them are missing still. Can you go back and see if you have some more?"

"Sure, no problem," he responded, but his tone indicated he was not sure where to look.

"Got a question, Dave," I began. "I have been looking at some of the documents, and they are huge. Most are 30 pages long or more, and you have 50-plus work instructions on how to clean the equipment. How do you keep those up-to-date?"

His answer was a critical one in my investigation.

"I don't," he admitted. "They were written for the audits and because I was told to do so. They were obsolete a couple of minutes after I finished writing them. The process and equipment change so much, it would be my full-time job just trying to revise them all. When a new employee starts, I will have them read the documents, but then the real training takes place on the floor."

"Thanks, Dave," I told him, as he walked to his car to head home after a long night.

I was starting to see the picture and what I thought was wrong. If you asked me at the time, I would not have been able to articulate the problem. It was a big one and one companies all over the world contend with time and time again.

Management Mini-Lesson: Nothing is to be done without a purpose. You are not there to please an auditor or even the FDA. You are there to make safe and high quality product for the consumer. Unless someone asks you to write things for this purpose, they are dead wrong.

THE CONNECTIONS WERE COMING INTO VIEW

Remember back to the start of the book and why philosophy is so important? This is why.

The quality system was written to meet an objective in the real world, to comply with the words of a standard. How it was addressed was a different story. The authors of the documents at the plant made a fatal error, which was why the plant did so poorly during the audit. They did not write their documents based on how things are actually done. They wrote their documents based on how they wished things were done. This was a critical error and one people make all the time.

They think of how they want something done in the perfect world that exists only in their minds. They think the only thing needed to make this world a reality is to write it down. Then, once this is complete, reality will snap into line. However, reality couldn't care less. "A is A"—reality is what it is. You need to find out what reality is and then begin to build your systems to reflect reality. Or, if you find the company's current reality is not the correct way of doing things, then—in certain areas of activity—you can make changes.

What type of areas can you change? Those of man's creation. However, you need to consider the physical parameters of reality when you define the areas you want to change
.

An example would be the amount of time you allow for a frozen ingredient to thaw. You can't thaw frozen peas, for example, in a room at ambient temperature, because this will cause areas on the outside to thaw first. The outside will be warm, and the inside will still be a block of frozen peas. Bacteria can grow on the outside part while you wait for the inside to catch up. This is reality, and it cannot be changed.

What you can do is respect this and thaw items in a cooler. It is slower, but you protect the peas from bacterial growth as the whole box slowly thaws over time. No wish of yours to have frozen peas to use in production *today* will speed up this thawing process. Your documents need to reflect this, and employees must be trained to understand not only how to do this, but why it needs to be done this way. Reality rules the day.

The man-made can be changed, but the rules of reality cannot. Gravity, thermodynamics, coefficients of friction, and everything we have discovered about the universe so far all come into play.

> Management Mini-Lesson: The man-made is what
> we can control, while respecting the rules of reality.
> You must understand the people and the process in
> this context if you want to manage it.

These were important lessons, and I was just beginning
to discover them for myself.

A NEW WAY

I knew the quality system at the plant was junk. I also
knew I had a year to fix it before the auditor returned.
The problem was, I didn't know what was wrong. I had an
inkling of what needed to be done, but my understanding of
philosophy was not yet there to guide me.

Everything you were supposed to do to have a good
quality system was there; it just didn't work. We had lots of
documents and lots of steps written down, but they didn't
connect with how things really worked in the plant. I had
begun to gather all the documents, and I printed them out,
so I could easily look at them. As I did, I would use a three
hole punch and put them in a binder on a small shelf I had
in my office. I arranged them first by author and then by area
of the plant they covered.

I had to move them after a couple of weeks because the
binders were full, and I needed more space. I eventually had
to order a new bookcase to hold them all. It was five levels
high and four feet or so wide. It was full of three ring binders
loaded with documents by the time I found everything.

No wonder we did so poorly on the audit! Who could
follow all the stuff written in these pages!

It boggled my mind—and the normal response to a

bad audit would be to write MORE documents. I knew something was wrong. I just didn't know what. I also knew figuring it out would be a pivotal moment in my career, the type of thing that would make or break me as a new quality assurance director.

Management Mini-Lesson: Don't EVER ignore the tell-tale signs of a disregard for reality. Follow them to the truth!

Help!

 The next step in figuring out this document mess was to get help from the plant floor. I needed someone who really understood how things actually worked in the plant. Someone who could explain to me how things really got done—because these documents in my office were not the answer. I had now read a lot of them, and every time I did, my eyes glazed over.

They were gigantic. Each document had an introduction, a section of definitions that could be as long as a page, a section on the scope of the document, and then a section describing the process in excruciating detail. As Dave had shown me in the sanitation work instructions, this section explained, step by step, how to perform a job in an area. I never saw these documents out on the floor when people were working, so what good were they?

I had given some thought about whom I would ask for help, and I chose someone not from quality, but a supervisor from out on the floor. She was very knowledgeable, and the people who worked for her liked her. Her shifts had the best quality and productivity results, and I knew she could help me figure this out.

I began to formulate a plan, and the first step was to figure out why the documentation system didn't work. I needed it to come back to reality.

Sitting down with the plant manager, I explained my proposal. It was a bold one. I wanted to revise the entire documentation system, starting from scratch. I knew this was tricky because this manager was a primary author of most of the documents, and I didn't want to insult him. I was going to dump his entire body of work from the previous five or more years.

"Phil," I started, "I want to dive into the reasons why we had a bad audit."

"Okay, what you are thinking?" he asked. His gaze was neutral, not revealing any irritation over what he thought was coming.

"The system is huge. Have you been in my office lately to see all the documents?" I inquired. "I have shown everyone who comes by, and they can't believe all the stuff we have to follow."

"Yes," he told me, "I have. I had no idea. Those were written over time, and as we found something we wanted to cover, I wrote another document. Man, they really add up."

"I agree," I gently stated. "That is why we need to really tear this apart and get to the reasons why the system isn't working. I don't want to add more documents. I think the answer is to remove a lot of them."

This got his attention.

"I think we can create an easier system to follow than what we have. I am not sure what it is, but I know what we have is not working. I need a favor from you to do this—I need some help," I explained.

He paused for a bit. Phil was a generally pretty easy to read visually. He gestured grandly, and if he disagreed with what you were saying, you knew it pretty quickly. Labor in the plant was tight, and resources to do things like this were not easy to come by. My ability to figure this out would not stop if he said no, but it would be severely retarded. It would take me a lot longer to figure this mystery out.

Management Mini-Lesson: Being a successful manager means you need to follow reality. A lot of times, this means pointing out unpleasant things to people who have more authority than you. Show them the data and point to why it needs to change. It's not personal, everyone wants to do a good job. Frame it that way and you'll be fine.

"What did you have in mind?" he stated in a business-like tone.

"I want to take Carmen off the floor and use her to help me out with this," I stated flat-out. "I need her expertise to help me understand what really takes place on the floor. She can help me match up how we actually do things with what we wrote incorrectly—the things we wished we did," I explained. This remark may have gone too far. This was mostly his system, and I didn't want to offend him, but this was the fact of the matter.

He looked at me for what seemed like forever. Finally, Phil responded, "Okay, you got it. This is important, and I support your plan. It's gonna put a strain on the rest of the team, but we can make it work. How long do you think you will need her?"

"I don't know, it may be a while. But, as soon as I gain an understanding, I can split her time, and she can help me a little less. But, in the beginning it will be full-time," I responded.

"Thanks, Phil, I really appreciate your support," I declared and then left his office.

Okay, I had what I needed, and now it was on Carmen and me to figure this thing out. But before I did, I wanted to spend a little time understanding my dilemma. If Carmen was to say yes and help me, I had to sell her on the idea. Simply telling her she was helping me would not give me someone who could really solve these issues. I needed a partner, not a subordinate.

A Ton of Work

I dove in and began to try and figure out what went wrong. I would read an instruction and then go out on the floor and watch what they were doing for a particular process. This really gets back to what we talked about earlier. Looking at reality was our first job. *Say what you do, and do what you say*, goes the old saying.

This was the informal version of Plan–Do–Check–Act.

I was acting like the auditor, trying to figure out the disconnects he saw. Was it because the people in the plant didn't want to follow the instructions, and the workers simply were bad? No, absolutely not. They wanted to do a good job, and they were doing everything in their power to do so.

Plants operate in shifts and generally you have two of them. One shift starts early in the morning, and the other goes late into the night. You have a point in the afternoon when the shifts change. I noticed when the second shift would come in, the operator of the machine would take over from the first shift and start messing with the settings.

This happened without fail—the new guy would always change all the settings on the machine, even when it was running perfectly. I would ask a question of him every time I saw this, an important question, but more to come on that in a bit. First, I needed to approach Carmen and get her on the team.

Did I Really Need Help?

Hell yes I did, but why did I pick someone from off the floor to work with? Carmen had no experience in quality assurance. She did write a few documents for her area, but nothing more than a few forms the people on the floor would fill out. She didn't have any technical skills for what I was looking to do. I sat looking at the documents in the bookcase next to my desk after another day on the floor talking with people.

This was the product of those who knew how to write documents. At least, that's what they thought. I was looking at the product of a mindset—a bunch of documents that didn't help move the business forward.

I chose Carmen exactly because she didn't have the same background. What I really needed was someone who was actually doing things on the floor and getting work done.

She got product out the door and did it well. She was the type of person who could help me figure out what was wrong with what we were doing.

The problem was—I hadn't yet asked her if she would help. She was a good-natured person, but this was a big commitment and a radical change in what she did—for what was most likely a significant period of time. Would she help me? There was, of course, only one way to find out.

"Hi Carmen, how are you today?" I asked in the cheeriest voice I could muster.

"Great, Bryan. What's up?"

"Can you come in my office for a sec?" I asked. This was never a good thing to hear from a director, and her face immediately reflected it.

"No, no this is a good thing!" I assured her, "Really!" I motioned her into my office. She followed after a slight pause.

She sat down in a chair in front of my desk. My office was small and off of the laboratory. A lot of people came and went, so it was a busy place.

"See all those binders?" I asked.

"Of course, kind of hard to miss all that."

"Yeah, it is. That is part of the problem. As you know, we just had our ISO audit, and we barely passed. I think the auditor saw we were really trying, but the documents were such a mess. Nothing we are actually doing matches up with what these things say," I shared. She nodded her head in agreement and kept her eyes on me. She was now curious as to what I was up to.

"Listen, I need to fix this, but I am not sure what is wrong. According to everything the experts say in Quality, we are doing the right stuff. But, it is not improving the business and not helping us make money. That scares the crap out of me."

"I agree, Bryan. I didn't even know this many documents existed. Is this really all from our ISO system?" she asked.

"Yep," I replied and let it sink in for a moment.

"Carmen, I need your help, your full-time help, in figuring out what is wrong," I revealed. This was it—I didn't want to make her do it. I needed her voluntary cooperation and her full engagement to tackle this.

"Why me?" she inquired. "You have people here in the lab who would be a lot better than me."

"I want your perspective. You are successful at what you do, and I need your mind to look at what we are doing here."

"Let me think about it. How long would this take?" she asked.

"Not sure," I admitted. "It could take a month, or it could take year. I have no idea."

"Okay, I will get back you tomorrow," she answered and left my office.

All I could do was wait. I felt vulnerable and wanted to make her do this. But I needed her willing participation if we were going to succeed. So, I waited.

Management Mini-Lesson: People need to understand why something needs to change. You need to explain the situation and gain their support. Remember, you can only control the people that report to you directly. The rest need to come on board to your plan voluntarily. Diplomacy is a valuable skill set you need to learn in any role.

DIVING IN

Well, as I'm sure you can guess, she accepted, and we dove into it. We began almost immediately. Carmen's normal duties were taken over by another supervisor who was none too happy about it, but it was what needed to be done.

The first thing to do was to talk with the authors and figure out how much they actually used from the documents. The best person to discuss this with was Dave, the sanitation manager. He had the most documents outside of quality assurance, and he wrote them himself. Dave was a big guy with a laid-back attitude, but he was a driver. If you asked Dave to do something and he said yes, you knew it would get done.

I pulled all the documents for sanitation from the bookcase and placed the binders on my desk. They took up almost a full row on the bookshelf, a significant amount to be sure.

"Hi Dave, thanks for meeting with us," I said. It was first thing in the morning, and he was just ending his night shift. Sanitation came in around 10 pm and worked until 6 or 7 am to get the plant ready for the next production day. It was a critical function for the company, and because of the hours he worked, Dave was largely unseen and taken for granted.

"I will try and keep this brief. I know you want to get home," I told him. He smiled and nodded his head in agreement.

"As you know from the opening meeting yesterday with the rest of the plant, we are revising the entire ISO system," I started. "The audit was a disaster, and the first thing we need to do is figure out why."

"Yeah, not a pretty sight."

"Anyway, your documents are the most detailed and I

wanted to start with yours," I stated. "Let me first ask an obvious question. Why?"

He tilted his head a little. It reminded me of when a dog hears a sound that confuses him. It was comical on the face of a man his size. "Not sure I follow," he responded.

"You wrote these for a reason. What was the reason?" I clarified. We had talked about this a little already, but I really wanted to drive the point home with him.

He paused before he answered, like the response would get him in trouble, "I wrote them because I was told to."

"Tell me more," I urged.

"The goal was to get ready for the audit, and I was told to write work instructions for my area. So, that's what I did. I was told to write them step by step on how to do everything. The more I wrote, the more I thought of, so the documents became bigger and bigger. Most of them are around 30 or so pages long," he explained. He was hitting his stride, and it was obvious he had a lot get to off his chest.

I whistled a little in affirmation and let him continue.

"Bryan, these documents helped a little, but not much," he confided, looking at the ceiling.

"I was told to write them so anyone would be able to come in off the street, read the work instruction, and do a job," he went on.

"Could they?" I asked, thinking of my first boss telling me the same thing. I hadn't thought about her in years, but it came back to me suddenly and very, very clearly. This was important, and it was the same thing Phil had recently repeated back to me as well.

Dave laughed. "No, of course, no one could. The instructions were inaccurate two days after I wrote them. Bryan, everything we do here changes so much. Equipment is updated, new ways of cleaning are put in place, and nothing ever stays the same. If I had to update these every time something changed, it would be all I ever did," he asserted.

"That is very interesting, Dave. Thank you. Let me ask you this: If the work instructions are wrong, how do your people know what to do?" I asked.

"Well, they do read them, on their first day at work," he said. "So, it's not like they are completely worthless. But then the real training begins."

"What happens then?" I asked.

"The new guy gets assigned to a mentor—someone I have trained who is really good at what they do. They teach the new person how to clean the filler," he easily answered. "That is where the training really takes place."

"Go on," I encouraged.

> Management Mini-Lesson: The ONLY way to find out what is really going on is to talk with the people who are actually doing it. Get their perspectives, things were done for a reason—right or wrong. Gather data and listen to people. You need allies if you are going to win the fight to make things right.

"After a week or so, I circle back with the trainer and ask how the new guy is doing. Really, I only get one of three answers. They go like this," he said.

1. "Dave, this guy is great. He has a good attitude and learns quickly. I think he will be ready to go out on his own next week."

2. "Dave, this guy is okay. He is nice, but slow. I have to repeat things a few times, but he eventually gets it.

He will do fine, but he is never going to be a superstar on the team."

3. "Dave, where did you find this guy? He has attitude, doesn't pay attention to what I am teaching, and tries to take shortcuts. I keep telling him the same thing over and over, but it doesn't seem to sink in. You should cut your losses, let him go, and find someone else."

Dave continued, "Once the evaluation from my trainer is in, I will go out to the floor and test the person myself. If they know what they are doing, they are part of my team. If not, we let them go and find someone else. I don't have time to babysit someone who can't pull their weight."

Well, now that was interesting.

I thanked Dave, and he left. Carmen and I sat and looked at each other. This conversation was not the first we had completed with other managers, but it was by far the most important. Something was there, but we were not sure what is was. It pointed to the reason why the system was broken.

"Our system is for show" was what came out of my mouth when I spoke to Carmen. "It does nothing and is only there to impress an auditor, the FDA, or our customers if they come to visit."

She nodded her head in agreement, adding, "Bryan, it's the same in my area on the floor. We wrote a bunch of stuff we don't use. I know we have work instructions for packaging and filling, but I couldn't tell you what they say. No one wants to admit it, and I just assumed I was the only one who felt that way."

I wanted to think about this for a while. I thanked Carmen, and she left my office. I pulled a sanitation work instruction and went over it. "Wow, this is awful," I thought as I read it. "This is exactly like the ones at my first job. Way,

way too much stuff here, and my eyes glaze over after a couple of pages. But what should it be?"

I pondered this for the rest of the week. I tried cutting down the length of the work instruction, but dropping out details didn't make it better. I needed a new perspective.

THE STORY THAT CHANGED EVERYTHING - THE BUS DRIVER PRINCIPLE

By chance, I read a story in a trade magazine from the American Society for Quality. That random act changed how I looked at this process and guides my work to this day. This is the story as I remember it.

Imagine you own a bus company.

You come in the office on a Monday morning to find out one of your best bus drivers has quit the company. Not the start to the week you were hoping for. You call in the human resources representative to begin the hiring process.

"Ruth," you start, "bad news. We need to replace Henry. He quit last Friday."

"Well, that's a bummer. I always liked him, nice guy. Want me to get started on finding a replacement?" asks Ruth.

"Yep, let's get going on this quickly. We are stretched thin enough as it is, and the other drivers are not going to be happy covering his route for very long," you say and let out a long sigh at the end.

"Well, let me know what you are looking for," Ruth inquires.

"The usual qualifications we need. Let's go over them for the ad." You relay the basic qualifications for the ad.

1. Experience driving the Transit Liner C-2 model bus

2. A clean commercial driving record

3. Available to work nights and weekends

4. Friendly and good with customers

5. Able to pass a drug test

6. Rate of pay depending on experience

The HR manager takes the information and creates an ad for the Internet and to post on some local job boards. Job applications come in at a pretty fast rate. Ruth reviews the applicants and picks the ones that have the right qualifications and are close to a match on the experience. She does some initial screening of candidates over the phone to weed out the ones who are not a fit. She narrows it down to three, and they come in to meet with you.

The first two are okay, with some decent qualifications, but one has an attitude and the other has driven other bus types, but not the type you are looking for. The need to fill this position fast means not a lot of time for training, so the second candidate is put into a backup slot with hopes the third will do better.

The third candidate comes into your office. "He at least went to the trouble of putting on a tie for the interview, that's a good sign," you think to yourself. "Maybe this one will be better."

"Come on in, and have a seat. My name is Bill," you say as you extend your hand to the candidate.

"Glad to meet you, Bill. My name is Frank," replies the candidate as he looks you in the eye and delivers a firm and practiced handshake—all good signs this interview is starting off on the right foot.

"Frank, thanks for coming in to talk with us today. Mind if we get right to it?" you say as you settle into your chair.

"Sounds great to me," responds Frank as he pulls out a notebook and pen.

"One of our best drivers quit unexpectedly two weeks

ago. His mother has been ill, and he had to go upstate and take care of her. Can't blame him, but it put us in a tough spot," you explain.

"I see, I am sorry to hear that," Frank comments.

"You resume is what we are looking for. I see you are familiar with the Transit Liner C-2. A good bus, but it can be finicky if you don't treat her right," you explain. "Driving record is good, right?" you ask.

"Yes," says Frank. "No tickets, accidents, or other problems. No DUIs either," he remarks.

"Excellent. Can you work weekends?" you ask.

"Absolutely, my wife actually prefers when I get out of the house. I like to keep busy, and I only live about ten minutes from here," answers Frank.

"Good to hear. I need to know: Why are you looking?" you ask.

"Well, I used to work for another bus company, and they went out of business. Moved down here after that to try and find some work, but I really do miss driving. It's nice to get out and talk with people. Too cooped up doing what I am up to now, working in a Home Depot," he explains.

"Perfect. Frank, I think you are the kind of guy we are looking for. When can you start?" you say with a smile as you extend your hand to him.

Frank does start, and he comes in on time. As you always do, you pair Frank with a veteran on your team. John has been driving buses for you for over ten years and is your most dependable worker. He has trained most of the people driving in the fleet, and you want him to do the same for Frank.

Frank and John meet the next day for training. After Ruth in HR takes care of a little paperwork, they dive right into it.

"Welcome aboard, Frank," John says with a smile. "You

are going to like it here. Friendly people, decent pay, and the team works together pretty good." Frank listens to him and slightly nods his head.

"I understand you have driven this model before, so let's get on the road and see how you handle her."

As they go out, John shows him the ropes. He gives him the route information, the hours of operation, where he can hit heavy traffic, what to do if he gets a flat, and everything else he is going to need to know when he drives the bus. After riding along for a couple of days, John is ready to report back to Bill.

"Hi John, how is the training going?" Bill asks.

"Great," replies John. "He is picking up everything really quickly, sharp guy."

"Excellent," Bill remarks. "Is he ready to go out on his own?"

"Yes," declares John. "He can handle it. We found a keeper with this guy."

"That is what I wanted to hear," Bill states. "Okay, he is on his own. Let's see how he does."

Frank is a little nervous at first, but he settles in quickly. A scuffle broke out on the bus one day, but he handled the situation exactly as he was trained to do. The company moves on, and everyone is happy.

This simple story was to become the focus of all my efforts in putting together my system.

Key Learnings

This sounds like a simple story that happens all the time, right? Well, yes and no. Some very key messages come out of this.

1. Workers are hired based on their skill set and company fit
2. Training takes place on the floor
3. New employee evaluation results fall in one of three scenarios:
   a. Good hire that can do the job, let them work on their own
      i. High level of trust
   b. Mediocre hire who can do the job with lots of direction, decide if you really need to keep them
      ii. Moderate level of trust, need to watch closely
   c. Bad hire that does not learn or has an attitude, don't keep
      iii. Low level of trust, will only work when prodded or watched

Hiring for the right skill level is very important. If every time you wanted to hire a new bus driver, you had to start from scratch, it would slow you down. The cost of hiring an experienced driver allows you to accelerate the learning cycle and have someone in place quickly who can do the job.

This was something absolutely critical, and when I read this story in the magazine, it was like a light went off in my head. The connections were made in my brain, and it was starting to make sense. Writing down steps in a document can never take the place of experience and hands-on training. The fatal flaw in the system was staring me in the face all along.

You can NEVER write a document that will be able take the place of training. You can NEVER write something that will be so detailed and exhaustive that someone can come in off the street and do a job. It is a pipe dream and something QA managers all over the world subscribe to. It does not work, and it cannot work. This is not reality. *You need to look at how things are done, and then write your documents to reflect what is really going on.* If you learn one thing from this book, this is it.

After I understood this flaw, I went back and looked at the documents Dave had created for sanitation. No wonder they failed!

The documents were not serving any purpose other than to capture how things were done at a particular point in time, but changes occur almost immediately after the writing is complete. In addition, the document is most likely written from the perspective of how the author would like the task done, not how it is really done. The document is almost immediately disconnected from the reality of how things are done in the plant.

Management Mini-Lesson: Documents must reflect reality. The second they don't, they need to be changed or discarded. Be ruthless in implementing this lesson.

This discovery led me to the second major insight into the documents. This one was very interesting because it was a paradox neither the industry nor anyone else doing this type of work had considered.

THE UNSEEN PARADOX

I went and looked at some more work instructions, and I realized something odd.

The work instructions were written to reflect the complexity of the task; the more complex the task being performed, the more complex the work instruction that written to support it. This is dead wrong. It is actually the opposite approach that is needed.

The most experienced people in a plant perform the most difficult tasks. They do not benefit from a long work instruction telling them what to do. They already know what to do, this is why they are doing the complex task! Ironic, isn't it?

If you need to tell an architect that the acronym "CADD" stands for "Computer Aided Design and Drafting" in a document, you are in trouble. She is not actually an architect and should not be doing that task. It's the same reason you spent your valuable time filling out an ad listing skills and interviewing people. New hires need a baseline of skills to perform a given job.

Another way to think of this is by taking it to an extreme. Have you ever seen a job description for the CEO of a company? Their job is extremely complicated, they have to juggle everything the company is doing and provide direction and vision for the entire organization. Everyone who works in that company is dependent on the thoughts and actions of one individual to make decisions that will impact the company, not only today, but decisions that may not be felt for years to come. How in the world do they do this? It requires years and years of experience by learning things the hard way earlier in their careers.

You can't teach that, you can only learn it yourself or from a mentor. A work instruction for a CEO would be beyond ridiculous; you might as well have one sentence which says, "Do everything today the company needs done." And leave it at that. So, why do we think it is different for anyone else?

I would like to be clear—it does work in the other direction as well. If you have employees with no experience involved in positions that need to be spelled out, they absolutely need work instructions listing every step of what is expected. They don't have the experience needed to do their jobs or make decisions on what to do. Their supervisor needs to oversee them closely and if the supervisor is not there, the employees can only operate within very tight constraints.

> Management Mini-Lesson: Take the context into consideration when creating a process document. Who is doing the process? Are they experienced or not? If so, what level of experience is needed? Do not write a process document simply to write it. That is a giant waste of time—and indicates a major, worrisome disconnect with reality.

GREAT, NOW WHAT?

Fine. So what do *experienced* people need in their work instructions? That was the next question in this process of discovery I needed to answer.

I decided to spend time on the plant floor to see if I could figure it out. I did, but it took a long time, and, like the other steps in the chain, it was right in front of me the whole time.

The company I worked for made a dairy product with a cheese base and ingredients added to it. They would make the cheese base and then add the ingredients to the mix to make different flavors. It was a really good product, and a lot of skill was needed to do it right.

In one large production room, we had the mixers and the fillers. The base cheese would be sent over from the make room, and the ingredients were added into a large kettle. The ingredients would then be mixed and tested. The next step was to send the mixture to the filling machines to dispense it into retail containers and be sealed. The finished product was then boxed and taken to the warehouse for cooling and shipping once it was released by quality assurance.

The machine that filled the cups was very old and difficult to run. Some of the most talented members of the production team ran these fillers. It was a hard job and required constant adjustment of the machine, depending on many factors. It was important to get the right texture and to fill the cup to the right level, at the same time.

The operator had to adjust for all kinds of factors, and one of the most important was temperature. If the mixture of cheese and ingredients was too hot or too cold, the machine could not compensate and the product would come out of the filler with the wrong texture, at which point the operator could only do so much to make it right.

I was watching this process one day, and I noticed a pattern develop over the course of the run. The batchers who were adding the ingredients to the cheese base were doing their job and sending the mix to the filling machines.

The operators at the filling machines were yelling at the batchers saying the cheese mixture was too cold. The batchers were yelling back it  was the operator's poor management of the machine causing the cheese to be cold, so they would just have to deal with it. This went on all day.

I looked at this and made an observation. The temperature of the cheese was beyond the control of the filling machine operator. They could do nothing to change it once it arrived; they were totally at the mercy of the batcher. The batcher had all the control, they could turn the heat on or off prior to sending the mixture to the filler. This relationship was one-way in relation to this standard.

I realized that the filler operator was the *customer* of

the batcher. They put in an order for a cheese mixture for packaging, and the batcher filled it. This changed everything, and it made clear who was responsible for what. The batcher was responsible, and they had the duty to send over the cheese mixture to the filler at the right temperature. If the cheese was not right, it was the batchers' fault! One side was holding the reins.

This was true throughout the entire process. The receivers brought in ingredients, the processors made cheese base with it, the batchers made the recipe, the fillers put it in a package, and then it went to the warehouse team who took it and shipped it to the customers. Everyone was dependent on the previous team in the process to do their job right. The filler had no control over temperature from the batcher. The batcher had no control over the moisture level of the cheese base. The processor had no control over the quality of the milk they were using, and so on.

This is what was missing from the work instructions. *What is it that you control and what range should it be in?* The next logical question came from this question. *What do you do about it if—for example—you are not at the right temperature?* I now had something to work with.

> Management Mini-Lesson: A manager needs to see the whole process, but in terms of the people in the process and how they impact each other. Most quality documents only look at the process and fail to see the hand-offs between the groups involved in the process.

A Man with a Plan

I set up a meeting with the batchers and the filler operators for this one process. My goal was to map it out and see if we could figure out the relationship between the two.

I focused on the things the batcher needed to do. They were worried about obtaining the following things to make a good batch of cheese mix:

1. Cheese in standard from the processors
2. Ingredients ready to go, to add to the mix
3. Cheese in a temperature range that allows for mixing
4. Time to mix the ingredients

So, we set up a work instruction that set the ranges of what was allowable to make good cheese with ingredients. Then we set up ranges for what it *should* be. So, for temperature of the cheese base coming over, it had to be between 175 and 185 degrees F—but this depended on the ingredients going into the mix.

The ingredients added would always change the temperature once you added them, so you needed to know this to make sure you were at a good temperature. The kettles could only heat, so you needed to be a little cooler, so you could bring up the temperature to the final target with a little heat. If it was too hot, you would have to wait for it to cool down, and this would cause the filler to shut down, so this was not good for production.

The temperature set was determined not by what the batcher thought it should be to make mixing easy; it was set by his "customer," the filler operator. In order to get the cheese to the right texture, you had a very narrow temperature window to hit. You were also made to take heat loss into account between the batching kettles and the filler. Not easy to do, and this is why they fought all day long. This was their attempt to try and get cheese that was the right temperature at the filler, but the batchers didn't necessarily understand why this was important.

It was now clear how things should work, at least with respect to this one relationship. The batcher had to send cheese to his "customer" at the desired temperature. If it was wrong, it was his fault. I wrote the works instructions to reflect this change in how we did things, and I trained the supervisor on how to manage this.

Let me state it again: If the temperature of the cheese at the filler was wrong, it was the fault of the batcher. He failed to meet the needs of his "customer," the filler operator.

Now that the roles were clear, the bickering and fighting went away. It was clear who was responsible for what and why. The next question was "What if the batcher couldn't get the cheese to the right temperature?"

That was interesting because something beyond the batchers' control was now being highlighted. Plants do not always run the way you want. You have mechanical failures and other issues that pop up. Cheese is too hot, ingredients are not thawed, and a million other little details can go wrong. Who is responsible for those? Reality was the first thing to look at.

When a line goes down, maintenance is called and the supervisor comes over to manage the process of getting the machine up and running again. They figure out what is wrong and get things going again. They are a supervisor because they know the process and the people on their team. Their job is to keep things running and on track. Sometimes they forget it is also their job to produce product that is in specification. This is where the work instructions come into play.

If things get out of whack, the supervisor steps in to fix

them. What if they can't? If the issue is too big, the operations manager is informed and they try to help out. This goes all the way up the chain, and if the problem is serious enough, a call to corporate headquarters may be needed. This process of escalation is normal and is how problems get fixed. Problems arise if the person who first notices an issue says nothing or the supervisor tells them to ignore it. The problem doesn't get fixed and doesn't go away. This is a recipe for disaster.

SPHERES OF RESPONSIBILITY

I named this process the *Spheres of Responsibility*. That means as an operator, I have a certain level of responsibility that I can act within. I can do things to run the process and keep things under control. I can adjust the filler speed, I can adjust the fill level, I can weigh the product to make sure it meets the label weight, but I can only do so much. If things like temperature are wrong, I can only let the batcher know it is wrong. I can only raise my hand and let the supervisor know what is going on. The issue is now theirs to investigate and fix.

They are a supervisor for a reason. They have a bigger box of tools to use to fix the issue. If they can't, it goes to the manger and so on. You don't need to write down anything beyond this in your work instruction because you are now relying on the expertise of the next person in the chain to solve the issue.

> Management Mini-Lesson: We all have a level of responsibility. It is our job to react to those parameters we can control and are trained to deal with. If we cannot bring those data points back into control, we need to let the next level of management know right away. If they can't fix it, it continues up the chain. The absolute wrong way is to ignore it—you can't fake reality.

So, the work instructions were coming together. The plant was divided into its main functions, and each person had measures for quality they were monitoring and actions to take if they fell out of those ranges.

I met with each area and learned the following:

1. Who does what in this process?
2. What are they measuring to control the quality of the product at that step in the process?
3. What are the ranges of measurement for the process?
4. What do they do if they fall out of those ranges?
5. What do they do if that doesn't work?

The only thing missing was a little guidance if things were drifting, but not seriously drifting yet. I defined these as issues that would not cause a complaint from our customers but would need to be corrected before they got worse. So, if the temperature from the kettle was drifting upwards, it would need to be brought down into range.

However, if it was suddenly really too hot, the guidance was to stop doing what you were doing. This was a point indicating a serious issue in need of an immediate correction.

This was a totally different concept for the plant to understand. What normally happened was product would be made, and you would go back after the fact and attempt to fix it. But by then it's too late; the damage has been done and the cost is now in the product.

This was really the worst possible way for a plant to operate. You would come into your office in the morning and find a part of a gasket from a food pipe on your desk in a baggie, along with a note for the product that it was used to make. Gaskets break and are food grade, but no one likes to find pieces in their food. So the question laid at my feet was always the same: Do we ship or not?

Management Mini-Lesson: You would think this process only applies to plants—and you would, of course, be wrong. Any department in the company--procurement, customer service, sales, etc. —can benefit from implementing Spheres of Responsibility. The person who can bring this process to their work and company will be seen as some kind of miracle-worker. You will know better than that, it's just reality.

Do We Ship or Not?

Product goes on hold if we have an issue. If we don't ship, we miss orders and customers are mad at us. If we ship, we run the risk that the broken gasket is in the product. It may not be in the product, but we are not sure if that is the case. So I would lead an investigation to find out where the gasket was most likely to be.

You usually had a little time before the product had to

ship to the customer--maybe a day at the most. You couldn't use technology to look for a missing gasket, because things like metal detectors and X-ray machines could not detect small pieces of rubber in the product. The pumps that move the cheese base grind everything that comes into them into very small pieces.

So, the decision came down to me. It was a no-win situation no matter what decision I made, because I was never sure. If it was a food safety issue, it was easy; the product stayed at the plant and was most likely destroyed. But those types of decisions were very rare.

By creating reality-based work instructions—as well as carefully (and accurately) defining all teams' spheres of influence—helped me clarify the process of handling these tricky situations. I had always assumed the decision belonged to quality because this was a "quality" defect. This was not true, I came to realize—it did not match the reality of the situation (yes, back to Aristotle). This was a failure of the process itself. The method of handling good ingredients in process material and packaged goods had failed. The trick now was to go back through the process and find out where the failure had occurred. The leadership to find this out lay with operations and the people making the product—not quality assurance.

Sure enough, a gasket showed up on my desk a couple of months later. Instead of accepting the premise that it was my responsibility to take the blame for the failure, I went to the office of the plant manager. Once in the office, I gave him the gasket piece and said product was on hold until his team could convince me that the remainder of the gasket was not in the product.

In reality, the gasket piece was not in the product. We had strainers and other systems in place to catch this type of problem. I would help in any way I could, but the responsibility was on his team to solve the issue and prevent it from happening again. Their process had failed to produce product acceptable to the consumer.

He just looked at me for a bit. This was new, and he wasn't quite sure how to respond. But he understood the change in psychology and began the investigation. He got up, thanked me, and went out to the floor to get the supervisor to begin figuring out where the gasket failure occurred. That was a good day.

> Management Mini-Lesson: Don't always assume that you own the problem. Find the source of the issue and work with them to resolve it. Part of being a good manager is making sure those with the responsibility exercise the authority to correct it—instead of just passing it off.

WORK INSTRUCTIONS AND THE NEW MANAGER MINDSET

Improving the work instructions was a long process that took us over a year and a half to figure out. The documents were all long, with sanitation documents leading the way at 30 plus pages each. The documents for the central processes (receiving, processing, packaging, and warehousing) were all in the neighborhood of ten plus pages of step by step instructions. By the time we were done, they were all down to four or so pages and included pictures of key steps in the process. The work instructions all had this same format:

1. Responsibilities for people in the process
2. List of trained personnel

3. Flowchart of the process

4. Basic description of the process

5. Key quality parameters, how to measure them and how often

6. The "green, yellow, and red" zones for each product

7. The actions taken for every range in a yellow or red zone.

The pictures included outputs of the process, such as pallet configurations at the end of the filling line, for example.

This was another very important shift with the work instructions, and one many companies struggle with. Supervisors in many cases become supervisors because they were good operators.

A good operator is defined as one that can run the line fast. So, they are promoted and think their job is to get everyone else to run the line fast. Their job is to run the line at the optimal speed that produces product that meets the needs of the consumer. Otherwise, they are just making garbage really fast.

> Management Mini-Lesson: Being a good manager is not about doing the things that made you a manager. This is in the past. Your job now is to guide people and help them to do their best. No one wins when the manager is just a high-paid operator.

Once we understood this simple, but easily overlooked, concept, it was a lot easier to work on issues. Just like the case of the gasket, it was clear who was responsible for making good product. It was the operator and the supervisor, not quality assurance—a simple concept that is easy to miss. This is reality, and it is a reality-oriented focus.

Now that we had these concepts in mind, my role was clear. It was not to sit in my office and write documents; it was to get with the operators and facilitate the process of understanding the output, what type of training needed to be done, what parameters were important for quality, what the drifts were and how to correct them, and what to do if things went wrong—in real time—on the line as soon as it happened.

Here is how the process worked. I would get together with the operators who ran a piece of equipment, let's say a filler. I would get the line data we normally gather, so I had a good idea of what type of tolerances the machine had before we began the meeting.

The next step was always the same. We would map out their specific section of the process. This was the handoff from where they got their materials to where they handed them off to the next person. This step was always interesting and also the part that took the most time.

Why did this take time to do? Because people automate what they do once they become good at it. It's like driving a car. When you first start driving, you have to mentally remember each step of the process and act it out. Your body is not used to the new stimulus, and your muscles are awkward in carrying out your commands. The car lurches as you hit the gas, and you may jerk the wheel too far when you want to turn. It's embarrassing, and it takes time.

But, after a while, it's a little easier. You can hit the gas smoothly and brake evenly when you approach a stop sign. After a while, you can even turn on the radio while you are driving. our confidence grows. The instructor is with you each step of the way and knows this is just part of learning how to drive. Eventually you get so good that your mind can drift, and you reach home some days not even sure how you got there.

This is the same with your job. After a while, you automate it. I needed to help my employees to "de-automate" it, dragging every little detail out of the process, and then distill it down to the basics of what was needed for quality. The goal was not to create a step by step method for running the machine. Hell no! That is what I was getting away from. Rather, it was to find out what was important and figure out how to react to problems.

So, if you are running the filler, you have many buttons and knobs that need to be adjusted during the course of the day to run the machine correctly and produce cheese with the right texture. The mistake in the past was to try and write it all down. It doesn't matter. That's right, you heard me—it doesn't matter. *It doesn't matter.*

If the operator is trained by the supervisor and knows how to run the machine, all I care about for the work instruction is the output of the machine. If you work in quality and you are reading this, your brain just exploded. It is the complete opposite of what we are taught. Guess what? It doesn't work. More documents do not equal more quality.

> Management Mini-Lesson: More documents do not equal more quality.

Let that mini-lesson sink in. Read it again. It applies to any job you are documenting.

The filler operators are some of the most experienced people in the plant. They run a complicated machine and have done so, in some cases, for more than ten years. They don't need me to tell them how to do it. What they do need is an understanding of what is good, what is marginal, and what is bad—and what to do about it when it reaches those points.

Experience Is King

On this particular product, the texture is extremely important. We know this because our consumer surveys indicated this. Consumers would penalize product with bad texture more than anything else. It was critical for us to have the right texture for the product. So I didn't care what buttons were pushed and in what order to run the machine; I did care about the texture coming out the other side.

In the past, the plant attempted to control texture on the line. They had posters and pictures of good and bad product next to the line, but it didn't seem to help. More pictures were added but the result was the same, and the complaint rate responses to the survey were the same.

We took all the operators to the lab, and we trained with them. We took samples right from the line and ran tests right there. It was a simple test where you could run a spoon through the product and tell if the texture was right. If it was too soft, it would run off the cracker the consumer would dip into it. If it was too dry and crumbly, it would break the cracker as the consumer dipped into it. Both were bad scenarios for us.

When we explained this to the operators, they got it right away. We determined that testing every 15 minutes on the line was the right time to look at the texture. If they were having problems or it was the start of the production run, they would look at the texture almost constantly to get it right.

Now, when the operator was unsure of the texture, they would bring a sample to the quality lab and the lab would take a look. If quality was unsure, they would go work with the operator and keep a close eye on the product. If they thought it may be too wet or too dry, they would put it on hold for evaluation the next day to see how it set up. If it was terrible, the operator would actually shut down the line and stop making bad product. What a concept!

In the past, the operator would just keep the line running, and then we had a warehouse full of bad product we could not ship. We were just adding cost and not meeting orders—a bad situation all around, but because the supervisors in the past thought their job was to make product fast, no matter what, we would find ourselves in this situation.

The last step of the work instruction for the filling process was to have pictures of the pallet configurations that were at the end of the line. This was very specific. Why did we do this? Well, the people at the end of the line were the least experienced people in the plant. This was where you started out working on the floor. The filler operator oversaw their work and managed what they did. The palletizers were inexperienced and didn't know what to do, so the instructions were very specific, and they got a lot of supervision, so they wouldn't screw up. They were like the teenager just starting to drive.

We even had feet painted on the floor showing where they were supposed to stand, so they could stack the pallets correctly and not get hit by a forklift. The system was coming together.

So, let's summarize where we are.

A company or a plant carries out a series of processes.

The steps are—

1. You bring in raw materials (*receiving*).
2. You do something to them (*processing*).
3. You package them (*packaging*).
4. You store and ship them (*warehousing*).

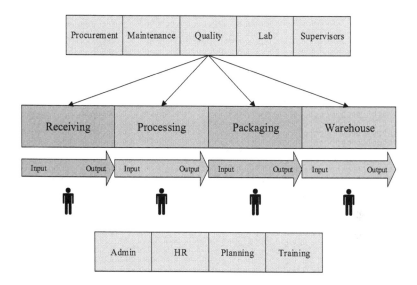

That's it. Every business does the same thing. It really doesn't matter where you work or what you do, you are part of this process whether you know it or not. The product may be data, it may be furniture, or it may be milk, but you follow this process.

Each step must follow the philosophical rules we have mentioned in the first section—

What is it?

What do I do about it?

This is reality, and it must be obeyed. Credit for this summary goes to the author, Sir Francis Bacon, who said, "Nature, to be commanded, must be obeyed."

The format for creating work instructions is included in the reference material at the end of the book.

TYING THIS ALL INTO A SYSTEM: THE HIERARCHY OF DOCUMENTS

This is great for a single work instruction, but how does this fit into the bigger picture?

All systems are arranged in a hierarchy. What is a hierarchy? It is simply an arrangement according to the elements of the standard in order of linkage to the principles of the standard. A hierarchy shows a linkage to why you have something, from a larger and smaller scale. Everything is there for a reason.

We been talking about the work instruction level, one that is pretty low down on the Documentation Pyramid.

In the graphic, documents that are high on the pyramid are more abstract. They are general concepts about your business. They support the documents lower in the pyramid by setting the context. If you can't say why you are doing something, then why do it?

Standard: The "rules of the game that your quality system is judged by. In this example, it is SQF (Safe Quality Foods). SQF is a set of food safety and quality rules that you are audited against. This is what the auditor uses to score you when she comes in to evaluate your plant.

Policy: These are general statements explaining why you are doing something. They don't really say how; they just put a stake in the ground.

Example: Here at XYZ Company, we only produce kosher products because we believe in producing high-quality meats for our customers.

It doesn't tell you what they do to be kosher; it just lays out the fact they are meeting a certain standard.

Procedure: A document that tells you how to do something. This is generally a document which impacts more than one person or department. It is how people in a process do something.

Example: A procedure that you have in place at the plant to verify that your ingredients are kosher. It would involve activities from both the receiving and quality manager.

Work Instruction: This is defined as an instruction for someone performing a task. It is specific, as shown in the main examples in the book so far.

Example: A work instruction on how to check incoming ingredients at receiving to make sure they are kosher before they are accepted into the plant.

Recording Form: This is the proof you actually did something, a written record of an activity you can check for compliance with a procedure or work instruction.

Example: The recording form the receiving clerk filled out when she did the incoming inspection for the kosher ingredients just received.

You can see how this is reality-focused to help manage your process based on how things operate in the real world.

The document hierarchy in the pyramid is a representation of this supporting structure. If you have a recording form, it is there to document what you did in a procedure or work instruction. The policy is why you did the work to begin with. The standard is what your entire system operates under.

Management Mini-Lesson: An overall system is based on a hierarchy which is reality-based. Documents are there for a specific reason and link to each other for an overall purpose, (in this case, the successful manufacture of food that makes the consumer happy).

How to Arrange Your Documents

Now that you have your documents, you can arrange them into what I refer to as a "document matrix." This is critical because it matches up the documents you have with what a standard is asking you to do.

We have all kinds of standards in business that we must follow. In quality, you have standards like safe quality foods (SQF), ISO, and other examples. These standards are a guidebook of the programs and elements you need to have in place to not only have a good manufacturing environment, but a good company as well.

They tell you the rules of the game, and if you want to be certified to their standard, you need to follow their rules. If you choose to be certified to SQF, then you pay a fee and they send out auditors to see if you are following the system they have put in place.

This document system shows an overall linkage back to what you do and keeps you grounded on what you should be focusing on in the organization. If you use it, you will find a lot of the things you used to do are not needed. They were most likely put in place for something that was important ten years ago, but no one cares about them any more. If it does not match up with the reality of how your company does business now, get rid of it!

The general rule of thumb I have found over the years of doing this is fully 60% of the documents and recorded processes in a company are not needed or are no longer followed. Removing these makes everyone's lives a lot easier.

> Management Mini-Lesson: Documents serve a purpose and nothing more. If they no longer meet that need, change them or get rid of them! They aren't the Dead Sea Scrolls, so trash them if you don't need them!

VALIDATION OF YOUR WORK

When an auditor looks at your systems, the conversation is very easy and goes likes this.

"Under the requirements of section 2.2 of the audit, you are required to have a method to control documents in your company to make sure everyone has the correct information," says the auditor.

"Absolutely," you reply. "We have a policy statement in our quality manual which states we follow the standards under section 2.2, and a person is designated as the document control administrator for the plant. We also a have procedure on how we do this. When we create a new document, we have a recording form we fill out to request a new document and a master list of all those documents. Which would you like to see first?"

This is auditor heaven. She asks a direct question, and you have a direct answer as to how you do it and evidence it is being done. She can look at the list of documents and compare it to what she sees in the plant. This makes life easy, and you can move on to the next section of the standard and the next requirement.

By this point in the book, this is an obvious way to do things. You look at reality, and you design a system to meet those requirements. However, this is not how most systems are developed or work. They are designed in a vacuum and are mostly a wish list of how the author would like things done. The audits for systems like this go down a very different path.

I have included more examples of this system approach with the bonus materials at the end of the book.

THE NEW MANAGER MINDSET PROCESS SUMMARY

Most people want to do a good job. They want to understand what to do and to leave work knowing the expectations were met.

In order to do this, they need to understand what those expectations are. Most people do not; they simply react to tasks and grind through the day. This is frustrating, to say the least.

ACTION PLAN: GAP ANALYSIS

You know the drill by now. I have attached a form to help you identify the processes in your area and to see what needs to be looked at. This is called a gap analysis, and it it will help you organize your thoughts in this area.

This is a big step, so a lot of people get overwhelmed. That's normal, don't let it worry you. If this was easy, it would already be done. The good news is a systematic approach allows you to see the big picture in terms of the consumer and lay out a plan to tackle it. You can do this!

CONCLUSION
APPLYING THIS TO YOU

How do you apply this to your area of work? Exactly the same as you do for quality and for your life in general. You look to reality. What is it you want to achieve?

If you are working in marketing, what is the standard you are using? Should you be making products that make the CEO happy, or should you be making products the consumer wants? How do you know what that is? Once you know, how do you communicate information to research and development, so they can design it?

If you work in accounting, you have very strict rules on how you can manage the finances of the company. What are those rules? What is the procedure you have in place for meeting those? How do you change those documents when an update in the law occurs? How do you document what you have done on recording forms or computer spreadsheets?

The same is true for IT. When an employee makes a help desk request, what is the work instruction you follow to make that happen? How are people assigned to the job and what is the priority they follow? How you do purchase equipment which meets the needs of the company?

At the executive level, how do you know if you are on the right track as a company? What procedures and measures do you have in place to show you are moving in the right direction?

These are all elements of one system, and they are based on looking out at the world, understanding what is needed, and then putting programs in place to do those activities. Then you record what you did so that you know you did it right.

The only additional action that will take your processes to the next level is to identify what you should do if things do not go as planned. What are the next steps and who at the next level in the company should be called in to assist with the solution?

Now that you have a system and you understand why you need one, you are ready for the last phase. None of this works unless you have the right people in place to help you organize your area of responsibility. The next section is how to find the best people you can--those who have not only the skill set but also the right attitudes to reach the goals of the organization.

UP NEXT

The next step in our journey together will help you to see that the people you surround yourself with to help you accomplish this task will make all the difference. The people we work with are the lifeblood of what we do—both inside and outside of the company. Find the best people and don't settle. I will teach you all I have learned about this important and never taught skill that all managers must have.

SECTION FOUR
PEOPLE AND DEVELOPMENT: PIVOT POINTS

All that is valuable in human society depends upon the opportunity for development accorded the individual.

—*Albert Einstein*

THE PEOPLE ARE KEY

Nothing we have gone over so far means anything without the most important part—people. People are the ones who make product, keep balance sheets healthy, and meet with the customers to make the business run. We often think all you need is equipment, especially in a plant. The machines only make it easier to make the product but without skilled people running them, they are so much metal, Teflon, and plastic.

Hiring—The Most Important Job You Do

Whenever I hire a new QA manager, I always tell them their job breaks down into two main areas. And let me reiterate—no matter what type of business you are managing, I am certain my discernment here applies, so please take notes.

Area One: Product

The product we make must always meet two criteria. The first is quality. The product must look, taste, and smell exactly like the consumer expects. This is the standard consumers hold in their heads. We must understand what that standard is and then maintain it. The second is food safety. Product must always be handled and maintained so it will never cause harm to a consumer. People assume the second one is always true, and if you violate it, you are in serious trouble.

Area Two: People

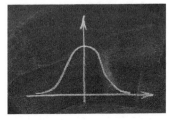

Your job is to understand the people in the plant and how they view their work. The easiest way to do this is what is referred to as my 10/80/10 rule. The ratio of the numbers doesn't matter that much; it's more the concept than anything else.

Eighty percent of the workforce is happy doing what they do. They come into work, do a good job, take direction, and go home at night. They go to their kids' soccer games on weekends, and life is good. That's great; we need people who are like this. They are critical and help make the plant run well.

The top ten percent are the ones who are not satisfied with the status quo. They will question how things are done;

they will be creative and find improvements for processes but will also become easily bored. These people should be your focus. Find them and challenge them. Give them new opportunities to grow and expand. Develop their careers and look for ways to promote them if they flourish. If you don't, they will leave the company and you will be much worse off.

The bottom ten percent (it's much lower, but I like symmetry) of the bell curve is usually easy to find. They are the ones who are looking to cheat the system. They are the ones who will clock in early, take extra breaks, and will work as little as possible. They take every sick day they can and will make life harder for those around them. They constantly complain about something and expect a reward before they do something, instead of afterward.

They are difficult, but the reason for concern is that if they feel slighted, they will take steps to damage the company. They will seek revenge. These people need to be found and asked to find employment elsewhere. They are a cancer in the plant or any other area of the business they touch.

THE INTERVIEW PROCESS

When hiring people, the absolute best way is by referral from someone you trust. Ideally, they were referred by a former employee who knows of someone who is looking. They have had the chance to work with the referred person day in and day out, and know their reputation is something they don't just put on for show. These are the people who stay around and help you reach new levels of success. Time to evaluate a person's performance is a luxury you normally don't have when hiring someone. A referral is a golden opportunity to understand someone's performance over an extended period.

> Management Mini-Lesson: When looking to hire someone, referrals made by those whom you trust are golden opportunities.

The Screening Process

The first step is a resume review. Look at the overall structure first. Is it organized? Does it flow well? How many pages does it take for them to showcase their career? If you are looking at an experienced candidate, two pages are sufficient. One page is enough for an entry-level position. A resume is just an introduction; candidates don't need to tell you their life story. I have actually received resumes six or more pages long. Are you kidding me? I am not going to read that. I do not have the time, and it implies arrogance. Your career is not that important, or I would have heard of you already.

Here's a tip. Most resumes are written in Microsoft Word. Turn on the codes (the weird little "¶" symbol in the toolbar) and look at how the document is formatted. Does the candidate know how to use the basic tools in the program for formatting? You would be surprised how many people do not know how to use the program, even simple things like tabs and bullet points. If they can't use Word, their computer skills are most likely at a very low level.

Next is the tone of the resume. If they are applying for a leadership role, do they focus on individual achievements and tactical items? Do they simply regurgitate their job description and intersperse words like "strategically" and "mentored" throughout the document? You want someone who can show results. I already know what a QA director does, so regurgitating your job description is not helpful or necessary. Show me your results and how you bring people together to get results. Actual outcomes speak volumes here.

Take your time and be picky on whom you select to talk to. The person you bring on board is someone you will be working with closely. As entrepreneur and author Jim Rohn famously noted, "You are the average of the five people you spend the most time with." Make sure you pick someone who is not only capable, but is a good person as well. You learn more from those around you than just skills.

The Phone Interview

Once you find people who are of interest to you, schedule a phone interview. You can use Skype as well, and this is an excellent tool to get more out of the discussion. It's more of a personal choice than anything else; use what you are comfortable with. Skype is a little harder because you have to dress up and play the part more. Take that into consideration. Make sure you have a private environment to talk with the candidate in and that your field of view is not distracting. If either end of the conversation has a slow Internet connection, do not use this option.

> Management Mini-Lesson: Start with a phone interview. Then do the in-person interview.

I still prefer the phone method for the first talk. You can take notes and not be as concerned with technical requirements, environmental considerations, and presentation. Schedule an hour for the call, and you should be the one who calls the candidate. This allows you to prepare and center yourself before the call. You need to be present in order to have a good conversation. This person requires all your attention, and you need to be there. So, turn off the phone or any other distraction, and be in a quiet place without distractions. Close your office door or go to a private room.

Schedule an hour for the chat. Don't tell them how long you have, but the call should go no longer than that. The reason will become apparent later on. You have two main types of interviews based on the level you are hiring for, but it is really a change in what you focus on.

Have a list of prepared questions ready to refer to if you need them. You can find some really great lists of questions on the Internet. You should mix in some direct and open-ended questions.

Open-ended questions work great for determining if someone really knows their work. The further you dig into the details of how they do something, the more detail they will provide. If they didn't really do it or have stretched their responsibility in an area, it will become obvious.

Lower Level Responsibility: This is a position where the candidate will take a lot of direction from a supervisor or another worker. In the interview, focus mainly on task execution and then on how they get along with others. The mix should be around 60/40.

Higher Level Responsibility: This candidate is the supervisor or leader giving direction. This conversation is more on the execution side and how you get things done. How tasks are done on an individual level is secondary. The ratio of 60/40 in this situation is a minimum. It gets even more lopsided the higher up the position is in the organization.

"LET'S HAVE A CHAT"

When you first start talking with the candidate, try and put them at ease. Start off with a little small talk, such as the weather or anything of that nature. Try and begin this as if you were meeting someone new at a personal gathering. Put them at ease and let them know you are easy to talk with.

Then lay out the agenda. Again, I would not mention how long you have to talk. You have blocked off an hour, but if you want to cut it short, you don't want them to worry about it. Also let them know this is a two-way street. You are hiring someone to help you, but it is just as important that they feel like this is a good match for them. It is really like dating. Do both sides like each other and want to spend time together?

If you have any issues with your company that could be concerning, be upfront about them. If the stock price recently went down, see if the candidate is aware of this and then explain why you think this is the case. It doesn't have to be the official company version, just your interpretation of events. People will be put at ease and less anxious about such things if someone on the inside can be transparent about the concern. No company is perfect, and you are hiring them to help improve it.

Emphasize that you want them to ask questions any time they want. I also save time at the end to allow the candidate to ask me questions and to go over any other areas they would like to know more about.

During the closeout, I always thank them for their time. I let them know we will be reaching out to the candidates we want to talk with further, regarding next steps. The next step almost always involves bringing them in for a face-to-face meeting. The phone screen is just to gauge fit; the in-person meeting tells a lot more about the candidate.

After the initial phone screen, go back over your notes and consider your thoughts. Have a sheet prepared that you use to evaluate the candidate. I have attached a good one at the end of this book for your use. It is one example which works well for me, and you may find another that is better suited to your style.

Again, this is almost like a marriage. If this person reports to you, you will be spending a lot of time with them. You will get to know their moods and how they work. Make sure it is someone you want to work with. I have known plenty of intelligent people in my career who got the work done, but they were not pleasant people. What happens is you end up not reaching out to them when you should because they are such jerks to deal with. Personality is just as important as skill set, and both must be great to have a good hire.

Management Mini-Lesson: A hire is not just about intelligence and skills. Personality is very important too.

If you are hiring for a higher level position, you also need to consider the candidate's philosophical approach to their work and how they tackle problems and create solutions. This is the strategic side as opposed to the tactical approach. A problem can be tackled from many angles, and how you go about it is very important.

THE PHILOSOPHY OF THE HIRE

Everything ties back to philosophy. Their identification of issues and their approach show up here.

What is it?

What do I do about it?

How do they see the world and how do they interact with it?

Do they believe...

- The world is an unknowable place of mystery and shadow, controlled by hidden forces no one can know?

or . . .

- The world is a real place that is understandable and operates under principles we can understand if we use logic and reason to determine a course of action?

The latter is how to live, not only at work, but in your life outside work as well. Reality is real, and it is our job to figure it out and use our minds to have a successful and enjoyable life. The beliefs above are opposite ends of the poles, and most people operate somewhere in between. Which person would you rather work with? Which person would be understandable and consistent?

The further up in the company I hire someone for, the more I focus on the person and how they think-- versus the skills they have. They are sitting in front of me because they are successful and have the skills. I need to find out if they have the mindset in place that will take them higher in the company to solve bigger problems.

Management Mini-Lesson: A key part of the interview is gauging the interviewee's personal philosophy, whether it is reality-based or not. By asking "how" questions, you can determine the person's philosophy.

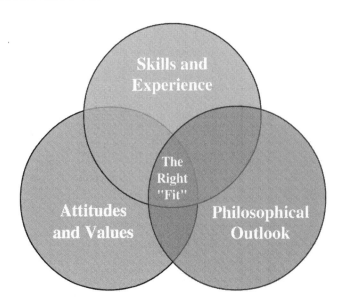

What does this mean? I look at *how* they decided to do something, not just that they did it. What was the basis for the decision? Did they do it just because their boss told them to? Did they do it as a reaction to an external stimulus? Did they think of the long-term implications of their actions?

It's ironic that if I am looking at a resume for a director or vice president position in a company and they list a lot of tactical skills on the document, I view it as a negative. I want to see *how* you do that, not *what* you do. Besides, you didn't do the work, someone else did.

The next step is to determine if they will fit in with the culture of the company. If you work for a very conservative company dressed in suits and ties (do they still exist?), then hiring a freewheeling hippie will be a disaster. If you work for a casual company that likes to have a little fun, then the opposite is true as well. Everyone you bring in will alter company culture a little bit, so if you like it the way it is, be wary of whom you bring into the family.

COME ON DOWN

The next step is to bring in the top candidates for a face-to-face meeting. As we discussed above, the phone call is great, but it is just the introduction. Some people use Skype or similar tools to blend in some face-to-face for the first round, but I prefer not to see candidates during the first contact. I don't want any physical sensory data to cloud my internal picture of them.

How many times have you said to someone after you meet, "Wow, you don't look anything like I pictured you in my mind"? This is not a bad thing; your mind is preparing a picture based on how they present themselves to you and how you are evaluating them. Better to wait and see how it matches up.

Make the travel for them as easy as possible. Don't fly them in the same day as the interview—too many things can go wrong on the trip, and you'll likely stress them out. Bring them in the night before, preferably a Sunday for a Monday interview. That way, everyone is fresh and in a position to put forward their best show. Don't schedule multiple candidates on the same day; there's no reason to do what used to be a tactic to raise competition between the candidates. It is not a competition between the two in the sense that they are really individuals who are matching up against an ideal person in your mind for the role.

I have the candidates meet with each person in the rotation individually, and I try to mix it up with responsibility and personality style if I can. One of the worst mistakes you can make when hiring people is to just hire people like you. If you are an analytical person, you love other analytical people. They make sense to you and have the same approach to life. What you may end up with is a bunch of people who can look at data all day long but never make a decision.

> Management Mini-Lesson: Don't always hire people who are just like you.

You should have them talk to four or so other people, in hour blocks. In between, take them to lunch and schedule time at the end of the day to wrap up with them. This is a good way to decompress the candidate and allow them to gather their thoughts. They just went through the wringer, so if you simply send them out the door, that feeling leaves with them. They take that stress with them until they hear from you, and it leaves a negative impression of the company with them. Send them away happy and with a feeling of appreciation for their time.

Plus, this is a perfect opportunity to see how they integrate their knowledge. What did they learn about the company? How do the people the candidate spoke with interact and make decisions? What are the main concerns of the group and how would the candidate put together a plan to help them? You get the idea.

One question I always ask every candidate is the following:

As you look back over your career to date, I see a lot of great things. So far, what would you list as the top three accomplishments you are most proud of?

This shows a couple of things. It shows if they have the ability to integrate and think long-term. What they pick is also important: is it tactical or a higher level improvement to a company? Is it a team member they mentored who was subsequently promoted?

You would be surprised how many people cannot answer this question or stumble around and simply rehash what they have already told me in the interview. It shows me whether they think in an organized manner or not. It's a simple question and very revealing when you think about your answers.

Try it—do it for yourself right now. Don't prepare—answer off the cuff.

What are the top three things you have done so far in your career that you are most proud of and why?

1. _____

2. _____

3. _____

Now look at what came to mind. Do you they fill you with a feeling of accomplishment? Do they make you smile when you think of them? If not, why? Are they big picture projects involving a lot of people or are they individual accomplishments? Are they work-related or more personal? These questions can tell you a lot about how you view yourself and the world.

You need to surround yourself with the best people to work with. This not only means intelligent individuals who are able to get the job done, it also means people you respect and admire. You want the whole package.

I am a fan of open-ended questions. I want a dialogue, not a terse answer to a specific question. You will find out more that way. If someone claims to have a big accomplishment under their belt, open-ended questions digging into the details will reveal if they were the leader of the project or simply a team member. They may not have had much involvement at all.

Open-Ended Question: Describe a situation in a project you were involved with that didn't go the way you expected. What did you do to correct it?

Closed-Ended Question: Have you used Microsoft Project before?

Which type of question will tell you more about the candidate and how they actually think?

When you are preparing for the interview, search on the Internet for some questions you can use that are relevant. I have a set I use which is included for your use in the appendix.

THE DECISION

The next day (don't wait, people forget what they think of the candidate) bring the whole team together for a face-to-face discussion regarding the candidate. Your questions should focus on

- Skill set and problem-solving
- Planning and long-term strategy
- Interactions with teams
- Management style
- Adaptability

Get the input of the entire team, ideally in a face-to-face meeting. You will be surprised to find that the person you thought was the leading candidate on the phone is usually not the one who shines once you meet them. In any event, keep all the candidates updated on the next steps and where you are in the process. If it's going to take a while, let them know.

> Management Mini-Lesson: Don't settle on a candidate who pretty much works. It's better to wait until you find a candidate you have great confidence in.

If you are not impressed by any of the candidates you bring in, that's fine, but DO NOT SETTLE. Bring in more candidates or start the screening process all over again. You do not want to hire someone that you are unsure of. If you do, it will cost you for many years to come--not only in money, but in frustration and missed opportunities as well.

THE OFFER

You have found the ideal candidate, good for you! If you did this correctly, they are as interested in you as you are in them. This is a two-way street, and both sides need to be happy. Entire books are written on just how to make an offer, but I like the simple approach. Come in with your best offer. Don't skimp and bring them in on the low end of the range. Pay as much as you can afford. You want them happy right off to bat. If they are high enough in the organization to get special perks, such as moving expenses or sign on bonuses, go for it.

Give them the offer in written form. You always need to do this. It will help make sure no misunderstandings take place. They may have heard more than what you actually said. Make sure they understand the terms, and if they have questions around benefits or similar topics, send them to the HR or benefits coordinator for an explanation. I also let the candidate know upfront that the offer I'm giving is my best. It is the most I can get.

Management Mini-Lesson: When you make the offer, don't skimp. Give as much as you can, provide it in written form, and let the person know it is your best offer.

If you do this, you avoid the headache of back and forth negotiation. They will always wonder if they could have gotten more. You also let them know you did everything possible to entice them to come work with you. This is only the beginning, and many other chances for advancement and raises are in the future if they fulfill the promise you have seen in them. I have yet to have a candidate push back once I explain my rationale.

Once they accept, set a reasonable start date. Don't force them to come in too soon. They need to leave their old job on good terms. If you are dealing with a lower level responsibility person, two weeks should be fine. Add weeks to the schedule depending on how far up the ladder you are hiring. Be reasonable and accommodating; it sets the tone for your future relationship.

Once they are on board, the training and development are just beginning.

CAREER DEVELOPMENT

Helping the people around you to advance is one the most satisfying things you can do in your job. When they get a promotion or big raise, you swell with pride because you were able to help them better themselves. It is always their choice to do so, but recognizing and assisting the worthy to rise is one of your main duties as a manager.

Don't forget. You are in this position because someone saw potential in you and helped you. No one is born into a job; someone has to give you a chance. When you get into a similar situation, do the same for others and help them as others once helped you.

So, we bring people into new roles. Sometimes they are qualified, other times they lack the real-world experience needed. This is not an exact art. We hope we hire people who can do the job, but the 10/80/10 rule still holds true. You want to find as many in the top tier as you can, but you can't really be sure what you have until they perform for a while. You need to see how they react to situations and not only handle accomplishments, but setbacks as well. What do they do when their project is stalled or even fails?

When a roadblock occurs, do they come to you looking for solution, or do they come to you with ideas already in hand, wanting only a recommendation on how to proceed? These types of thought processes indicate if the person is independent in their thinking. Philosophically, do they see the world as something that can be understood or as a mystery which requires guidance from another source?

Management Mini-Lesson: Remember, these rules and recommendations apply equally to your career as well. If you want to be promoted, follow these rules so that your boss can see your value, too.

MISSION AND VISION STATEMENTS, REVISITED

I always develop clear objectives for the department and for my team before the beginning of every year. This may or may not link up with the vision and mission of the company. Remember the Enron statement from earlier in the book? Frankly, mission and vision statements can just be an exercise in futility.

They are usually written so broadly that they can't be linked to anything. Here's a mission statement that leaves me scratching my head:

> *To help make every brand more inspiring,*
> *and the world more intelligent.*

Who was the company that wrote this confusing statement? Avery Dennison, makers of stick-on labels you put on your file folders at work. Really, "make the world more intelligent" with labels? They have received quite a bit of criticism over it, but yet it stubbornly remains in place on their website.

Mission and vision statements need to put a stake in the ground and help to define your company to the world. They also need to give direction to employees putting together goals and objectives in the organization. They are a philosophical statement to the world about the purpose of the company.

This helps in theory, but to be fair most of these statements do nothing. They are impossible to change, so other than seeing them in a few places around the office or on your website, they will most likely not impact your objective development process. Read them and nod your head in faux appreciation of their self-importance and move on.

The most important thing is to align your objectives with those of your boss and maybe one level higher.

If you don't have a formal process for objectives in your company, do it anyway! You will keep yourself and your team on track for the year and have a clear list of accomplishments when it comes review time. Plus, your initiative may even be adopted into the organization beyond your department. That's a nice little feather in your cap!

> Management Mini-Lesson: Even if your company does not have a formal objective process, make one for yourself and your team anyway.

Objectives should focus on three main areas:

1. Strategic objectives
2. Tactical objectives
3. Development objectives

I have included a template I use that works well in helping you articulate your objectives in these three areas.

STRATEGIC OBJECTIVES

These are the main things you want to accomplish over the next year in your department. These should be looked at in terms of the big buckets of work—audits, process development, key performance development, and other big projects you will be working on. This is not a rehash of your job description. You are telling your boss what you and your team think is important. If your boss disagrees, you need to find out right away. Otherwise, you could spend a lot of resources working on things your boss doesn't think are important.

These can be written broadly and not necessarily with specific measures.

Here is an example:

Identify a new process for product development and provide recommendations to senior management.

This is a big goal for your objectives which requires many people outside of your control to push it through. The most you can promise is that you will put together a plan and make a recommendation. The organization may not be ready or willing to implement it. So, write the objective in a way that recognizes this fact.

TACTICAL OBJECTIVES

This is the next level of granularity. Here, you are showing measurable activities which you can check off your list as you accomplish them over the year. You want a mix of strategic and tactical targets showing your ability to think in terms of your department as well as the larger goals of the company.

Example:

In quarter one, kick off a project team to develop the stage gate process for product development. Select and then train an interdepartmental team in that process.

This is specific. You can show your boss this was done and provide evidence. Doing what you say is the key outcome here. You want to be known as someone who can set objectives and reach them. If the company changes course and this is removed from your plate as a body of work that needs to be done, you have a reason why it was not done. People forget by the time your review comes up, so it is important to document for the time when it does comes up.

The overall thought here is one that goes both up and down the chain of command. This is a general principle and works in many applications, so burn this phrase into your consciousness—

No one likes to be surprised.

Management Mini-Lesson: Make sure your employees know what is expected of them. Your boss needs to know what you are up to as well.

If the boss is unsure of what you are doing and trust is not present, they will bug you to find out what you are up to. This cuts into your available time to get things done.

Hold quarterly objective review meetings with your team. Sit down with them or have a conference call if they are remote. Have them fill out their accomplishments for the quarter and be prepared to go over them with you. Things change, and this is the time to refresh objectives to see if they are still relevant. This is not a static document you create at the beginning of the year and file away. Use it like it was meant to be used.

This applies to your boss as well. If the boss doesn't schedule a quarterly meeting with you, ask if he or she would like one. If not, update your objectives and send them to the boss. Remember, no surprises.

I also have an attachment I use to help track the development of my team on a personal level. This individual development plan is a listing of the things the team members determine they want to get better at. I budget around 2,000 dollars per person for this, including for me.

I have attached a copy of what I use.

What new skills do they want to develop? Maybe brush

up on Excel or attend an online seminar? These are all things that relate to their job or even skills they may need for their next advancement. It is up to them to pick, and the dollar limit helps to identify how wisely they allocate their funds. Traveling to a conference will burn up most of that money.

If you take classes via Skype over the Internet, you can do a lot more. This is a good exercise in budgeting for team members who may not get much exposure to other sides of the business. You, of course, retain veto power over proposals and what is actually included. No, a trip to Las Vegas in order to understand statistics via the roulette table is not a good use of company funds.

The bottom line here is when it comes time for reviews and salary recommendations for next year, expectations need to be clear. Did they meet or exceed their goals? Did they do the minimum or branch off into new areas of knowledge? If you are going to push for a big raise or promotion for that employee, you need the ammunition to plead your case with HR and your boss. These are tight times, and there is only a limited amount of money to go around. If the employee deserves it, make sure you have a solid case.

When you sit down to give your team member their review, it should really be a very quick process. Mine usually take no longer than 15 minutes. They already know how they did, and if something comes up unexpectedly, you did a bad job of communicating with them. Congratulations! You have identified a development opportunity for yourself in the coming year.

The same applies for your boss. Give him or her the information needed in writing and sit down with him or her on a quarterly basis too. Bosses are busy people, looking at problems at a wider scale than you are, so help them out. It is so easy to forget what you have done over the course of a year, so imagine what it is like for your boss. Can you remember what you did six months ago? Your boss surely cannot either.

Blind Spots

As we discussed in Section One, everyone has blind spots. These are areas where you have weaknesses, but you are unaware they exist. It's no secret to everyone you work with or know. They see your weak areas right away. You can go to a meeting with a group of strangers, and they will pick up on them too. It's not a bad thing; it's just part of who you are and who anybody is. But you need feedback from other people for you to be aware of these areas of your personality.

For example, remember how I told you my blind spot is the scowling face I unintentionally make when I work at the computer? I had no idea I was doing this, and it took some feedback to let me know this is how people saw me. I am still this way, but I am now more aware. I try and tell those who don't know me about it, or if someone comes by to see me, I am aware of the pattern and break it when they arrive.

Awareness is the key here; notice things that people pick up on and modify those responses. This means you will need to be open and provide opportunities for employees to give you feedback.

> Management Mini-Lesson: Be sure to provide opportunities for your employees to give you feedback.

Always remember people like consistency. They like to know what to expect. If you are fair and the rules of the game are laid out in front of them, they know when they are not meeting expectations. Identify it when it occurs and help them get back on track. Don't dodge the issue and pretend it's okay. It's not. It will grow and lead to lapses in other areas. Have the discussion and get them back on track. Remember, your main job now is overseeing your people. You have moved from tasks to management. Don't let the day-to-day blind you to your team and what they need. If you neglect them, they will go elsewhere.

What People Need

Let's tie this back to discussions about what people need. Two key factors are absolutely critical for any job, and employees crave this for their roles. If you give this to them, you will be a fantastic boss:

1. Training
2. Work instructions

As I highlighted in my own work experiences, training is critical and breaks into two main areas:

1. Things everyone needs
2. Objectives specific for the role

For example, a new line operator for the plant is starting next Monday. The first thing she is going to do is go to human resources at the corporate headquarters to go over company training. She will get a manual with all the company policies and procedures written in it. The HR manager will go over important topics in the manual to make sure the new employee was informed of these items. Specific training around sexual harassment or other topics usually takes place. Then, employees get the stuff they need to do their job from IT. A company phone, computer keys, and other such things are issued to them.

The next few days they dive into the specifics. They go

to their work area (in this case, the plant) and get settled into their new work environment. They get an office, more keys, and training specific to the plant. They get training in emergency evacuation and other similar processes from HR.

In other words, they get training everyone needs. This is a familiar story to anyone who has worked for a company.

The real training is the next part, and it is what we talked about with the Bus Driver Principle story. The new person is assigned a trainer to show them the ropes of life in the plant. The trainer teaches them the details of life there—who reports to whom, how the shifts operate, what type of products they make, and all the high level items. Actual training takes place on the machines and how they work. The tricks and tips the trainer has picked up over the years are communicated to the newbie. The trainer also needs to tell them what to do when things go wrong and how the escalation process works in the plant.

A period of time passes when the hands-on training takes place. Once the trainer is comfortable and the management agrees, the newbie is pushed out of the nest. This is a measure of the training ability of the mentor and the adaptability of the new employee. If all goes well, some corrections take place, and the trainee learns and becomes an independent operator in the plant.

Sound a little familiar? This is how we raise our children. We teach them the guard rails early in life, those things which can cause pain really quickly. After that, skills are taught and tested to see if the offspring understand the training. Once they are ready, they move out on their own with our oversight. Then they are on their own, raising their hands for help less and less frequently.

It's a great accomplishment for a parent, and when your trainee is successful in the new role, the pride is the same.

That is the feeling of helping another person to succeed in life and learn a new ability. It is one of the great joys in life.

It's why I wrote this book—I want to help you succeed and give you the tools to do so.

The same is true when you are able to help someone advance and get a promotion. It may be with the company you are in, or it may be a move to another. That's okay. Once you get to a certain level, you almost always have to leave to reach the next level. You are still there for this person no matter where you work.

In my field of work, a major part of what I do is food safety. It's a huge responsibility to make sure the food people eat is always safe. It covers almost everything in a company to make sure the company is thinking of the safety of its consumers in everything the employees do.

I saw a presentation once from the head of food safety for Jack in the Box. As I already mentioned in Section Two, this company had a terrible food safety problem caused by hamburgers that were undercooked. Four children died as a result.

It was a terrible tragedy that could have been easily avoided. A phrase came up from this person that has guided my career to this day.

She said, "At Jack in the Box, food safety is not a point of competition. If you come to our company, we will show you all we do to make sure the consumer is safe."

The phrasing may not be exact, but it was exactly right. Food safety is the concern of everyone in the food industry, and I share all I have learned in my career freely with those who would like to know. If one company fails, we all fail and trust is lost with the consumer in the food supply.

Trust is all we have, and we assume what we eat is safe every day. No one goes to the grocery store and asks about the companies that made the food sitting on the shelves. It is just assumed we did our jobs as manufacturers to keep people safe. We usually do, but sometimes mistakes happen. It is our job to share our learnings with everyone who is responsible for food safety to help prevent it from happening again.

My discipline has a loyalty beyond the company that writes us our checks. There are lines that cannot be crossed to ensure the integrity of the company is maintained, but food safety is universal, and I will do what I can to help anyone who asks.

Think this way in your job. How can I do better not only for this company, but for my profession in general? What improvements can be made to enhance what we do? Find mentors and people who are further down the path from you and learn from them. They can shave years of pain and frustration off your journey. Your job can be lonely, so find people who are in your shoes and help each other succeed.

Remember earlier when I said one of the things I look for in new employees is the ability to think strategically? This is how you get there.

CONCLUSION

There is no going back now.

For better or for worse, you now know how to succeed in your career as a manager. You have the tools and understand how to get things done better than almost everyone you come into contact with.

The New Manager Mindset is a way of thinking. It is a way of integrating your knowledge in four main areas—philosophy, the consumer, systems, and people—to do your job well and influence the organization in the right direction. With your insight, your business can be far better than anyone ever thought it could be.

That's great—but the best part is how you will be able to help others do the same. You will be able to develop a team you will enjoy working with. A team of people who care and want to help build your company as well. People who will share your values and whom you can call your friends.

It only takes a few people to change any culture. It is the thinkers and doers who create this change. They are the 10% at the right of the bell curve who make a difference. They are the ones who think outside the box and bring improvement. Most of these phrases are mere abstractions for the 80% in the middle. The 10% at the bottom fear them. You need to know who is who, and now you can.

You can think about the four elements of management in terms of the value you bring to the table and the purpose of you and your team in the organization.

Philosophy – Understanding why things are of value to people

Consumer – Creating the right value proposition for consumers

Systems – Uniform methods for making value via employees

People – Teams that create value, for themselves and for the consumer

Teach others what you have learned here. Knowledge without implementation is just data. Talk it over, do it in stages, and challenge it. If you come up with better ways and new insights, tell me! This is an evolving system, and it can always be better. My contact information is at the end of the book.

We are better together, so reach out to me and let's install the New Manager Mindset in as many businesses as possible. These systems are revolutionary and can change the world for the better.

Let's share them with the world—it's time.

ACTION PLAN: HIRING AND LEADING YOUR TEAM

Review the reference information. It includes templates and other information to help you find the right people on your journey and create a clear path for your team. These people look to you for leadership, so be out in front and show them the way. Leaders lead the way, jumping out of the trenches and charging ahead. We don't always have the answers, but we know reality will show us the correct path. We just need the right tools and methods of thinking to get us there.

Don't do this on your own. Learn from others and develop the concepts presented here. Challenge it, expand it and make it yours. Everything must grow and improve if it is to remain valuable.

My contact information is at the beginning and end of this book. Reach out, I would love to hear what you have learned!

REFERENCE MATERIAL

PHILOSOPHY OF BUSINESS

Start with Why TED Talk - Simon Sinek: http://tinyurl.com/ovuxymt

Simon's author page on Amazon: http://tinyurl.com/pdh7c2p

Getting Things Done - David Allen: http://gettingthingsdone.com/

David's author page on Amazon: http://tinyurl.com/jyzmchc

THE CONSUMER

Diet Coke Case Story: https://en.wikipedia.org/wiki/New_Coke

Tylenol Case Study: http://www.ou.edu/deptcomm/dodjcc/groups/02C2/Johnson%20&%20Johnson.htm

QUALITY SYSTEMS

Jack in the Box Case Study: http://tinyurl.com/jt9jg9w

Marler Clark Law Firm Jack in the Box: http://tinyurl.com/yh8yv4u

Firestone Case Study: https://en.wikipedia.org/wiki/Firestone_and_Ford_tire_controversy

Example Hierarchy Matrix: http://tinyurl.com/zzgtl2t

Example Policy Template: http://tinyurl.com/qj4bzpu

Example Procedure Template: http://tinyurl.com/gwyt2ba

Example Work Instruction Template: http://tinyurl.com/z35fro9

Example Recording Form Template: http://tinyurl.com/hyw8g7k

Example Table Template: http://tinyurl.com/hdkln6y

SQFI Website: http://www.sqfi.com/

PEOPLE DEVELOPMENT

Informational Interviews: http://tinyurl.com/p26vglx

Paul Slezak Interview Guide: http://tinyurl.com/ouksmzn

Interview Evaluation Form: http://tinyurl.com/jsdtxyb

Annual Development Plan and Objective Form: http://tinyurl.com/hsqv82l

HOW TO REACH ME

This book is the culmination of my life's work to date and can only be summarized. I would love to help you implement the subjects we have discussed in this book. Send me an email at bryan@newmanagermindset.com and I'll get back to you asap.

Thanks!

24569446R00111

Made in the USA
San Bernardino, CA
06 February 2019